"LEFT-WING" COMMUNISM AN INFANTILE DISORDER

V. I. LENIN

Paperback: 978-939574149-1

Printed by:

Sanage Publishing House LLP
Mumbai, India

sanagepublishing@gmail.com

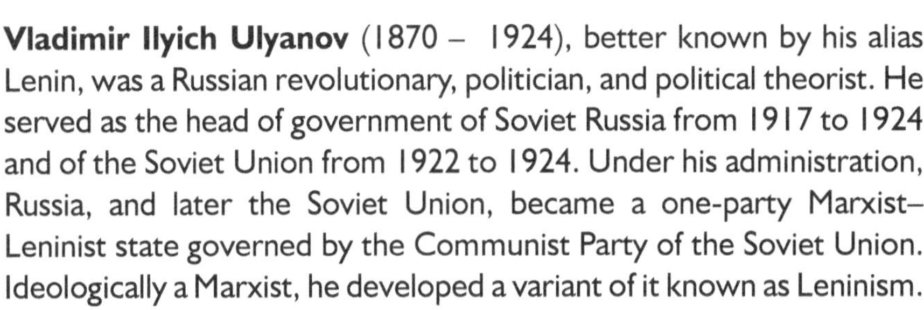

Vladimir Ilyich Ulyanov (1870 – 1924), better known by his alias Lenin, was a Russian revolutionary, politician, and political theorist. He served as the head of government of Soviet Russia from 1917 to 1924 and of the Soviet Union from 1922 to 1924. Under his administration, Russia, and later the Soviet Union, became a one-party Marxist–Leninist state governed by the Communist Party of the Soviet Union. Ideologically a Marxist, he developed a variant of it known as Leninism.

CONTENTS

In What Sense We Can Speak Of The International Significance Of The Russian Revolution

In the first months after the proletariat in Russia had won political power (October 25 [November 7], 1917), it might have seemed that the enormous difference between backward Russia and the advanced countries of Western Europe would lead to the proletarian revolution in the latter countries bearing very little resemblance to ours. We now possess quite considerable international experience, which shows very definitely that certain fundamental features of our revolution have a significance that is not local, or peculiarly national, or Russian alone, but international. I am not speaking here of international significance in the broad sense of the term: not merely several but all the primary features of our revolution, and many of its secondary features, are of international significance in the meaning of its effect: on all countries. I am speaking of it in the narrowest sense of the word, taking international significance to mean the international validity or the historical inevitability of a repetition, on an international scale, of what has taken place in our country. It must be admitted that certain fundamental features of our revolution do possess that significance.

It would, of course, be grossly erroneous to exaggerate this truth and to extend it beyond certain fundamental features of our revolution. It would also be erroneous to lose sight of the fact that, soon after the victory of the proletarian revolution in at least one of the advanced countries, a sharp change will probably come about: Russia will cease to be the model and will once again become a backward country (in the "Soviet" and the socialist sense).

At the present moment in history, however, it is the Russian model that reveals to all countries something and something highly significant of their near and inevitable future. Advanced workers in *all* lands have long realized this; more often than not, they have grasped it with their revolutionary class instinct rather than realized it. Herein lies the international "significance" (in the narrow sense of the word) of Soviet power, and of the fundamentals of Bolshevik theory and tactics. The "revolutionary" leaders of the Second International, such as Kautsky in Germany and Otto Bauer and Friedrich Adler in Austria, have failed to understand this, which is why they have proved to be reactionaries and advocates of the worst kind of opportunism and social treachery. Incidentally, the anonymous pamphlet entitled The World Revolution (*Weltrevolution)*, which appeared in Vienna in 1919 (*Sozialistische Bücherei*, Heft 11; Ignaz Brand), very clearly reveals their entire thinking and their entire range of ideas, or, rather, the full extent of their stupidity, pedantry, baseness, and betrayal of working-class interests and that, moreover, under the guise of "defending" the idea of "world revolution".

We shall, however, deal with this pamphlet in greater detail some other time. We shall here note only one more point: in bygone days, when he was still a Marxist and not a renegade, Kautsky, dealing with the question as an historian, foresaw the possibility of a situation arising in which the revolutionary spirit of the Russian proletariat would provide a model to Western Europe. This was in 1902, when Kautsky wrote an article for the revolutionary Iskra, [1] entitled "The Slavs and Revolution". Here is what he wrote in the article:

> "At the present time (in contrast with 1848) it would seem that not only have the Slavs entered the ranks of the revolutionary nations, but that the Centre of revolutionary thought and revolutionary action is shifting more and more

to the Slavs. The revolutionary Centre is shifting from the West to the East. In the first half of the nineteenth century, it was located in France, at times in England. In 1848 Germany too joined the ranks of the revolutionary nations. . . . The new century has begun with events which suggest the idea that we are approaching a further shift of the revolutionary Centre, namely, to Russia. . . . Russia, which has borrowed so much revolutionary initiative from the West, is now perhaps herself ready to serve the West as a source of revolutionary energy. The Russian revolutionary movement that is now flaring up will perhaps prove to be the most potent means of exorcising the spirit of flabby philistinism and coldly calculating politics that is beginning to spread in our midst, and it may cause the fighting spirit and the passionate devotion to our great ideals to flare up again. To Western Europe, Russia has long ceased to be a bulwark of reaction and absolutism. I think the reverse is true today. Western Europe is becoming Russia's bulwark of reaction and absolutism. . . . The Russian revolutionaries might perhaps have coped with the tsar long ago had they not been compelled at the same time to fight his ally—European capital. Let us hope that this time they will succeed in coping with both enemies, and that the new 'Holy Alliance' will collapse more rapidly than its predecessors did. However, the present struggle in Russia may end, the blood and suffering of the martyrs whom, unfortunately, it will produce in too great numbers, will not have been in vain. They will nourish the shoots of social revolution throughout the civilized world and make them grow more luxuriantly and rapidly. In 1848 the Slavs were a killing frost which blighted the flowers of the people's spring. Perhaps they are now destined to be the storm that will break the ice of reaction and irresistibly bring with it a new and happy spring for the nations" (Karl Kautsky, "The Slavs and Revolution", Iskra, Russian Social-

Democratic revolutionary newspaper, No. 18, March 10, 1902).

How well Karl Kautsky wrote eighteen years ago!

FOOTNOTES

[1] The old *Iskra*, the first illegal Marxist newspaper in Russia. It was founded by V. I. Lenin in 1900 and played a decisive role in the formation of a revolutionary Marxist party of the working class in Russia. *Iskra's* first issue appeared in Leipzig in December 1900, the following issues being brought out in Munich, and then beginning with July 1902 in London, and after the spring of 1903 in Geneva.

On Lenin's initiative and with his participation, the editorial staff drew up a draft of the Party's Programme (published in *Iskra* No. 21), and prepared the Second Congress of the R.S.D.L.P., at which the Russian revolutionary Marxist party was actually founded.

Soon after the Second Congress, the Mensheviks, supported by Plekhanov, won control of *Iskra*. Beginning with issue No. 52, *Iskra* ceased to be an organ of the revolutionary Marxists.

An Essential Condition Of The Bolsheviks' Success

It is, I think, almost universally realized at present that the Bolsheviks could not have retained power for two and a half months, let alone two and a half years, without the most rigorous and truly iron discipline in our Party, or without the fullest and unreserved support from the entire mass of the working class, that is, from all thinking, honest, devoted and influential elements in it, capable of leading the backward strata or carrying the latter along with them.

The dictatorship of the proletariat means a most determined and most ruthless war waged by the new class against a *more powerful* enemy, the bourgeoisie, whose resistance is increased *tenfold* by their overthrow (even if only in a single country), and whose power lies, not only in the strength of international capital, the strength and durability of their international connections, but also in the *force* of habit, in the strength of small-scale production. Unfortunately, small-scale production is still widespread in the world, and *small-scale production* engenders capitalism and the bourgeoisie continuously, daily, hourly, spontaneously, and on a mass scale. All these reasons make the dictatorship of the proletariat necessary, and victory over the bourgeoisie is impossible without a long, stubborn, and desperate life and death struggle which calls for tenacity, discipline, and a single and inflexible will.

I repeat: the experience of the victorious dictatorship of the proletariat in Russia has clearly shown even to those who are incapable of thinking or have had no occasion to give thought to the matter that absolute centralization and rigorous discipline of the proletariat are an essential condition of victory over the bourgeoisie.

This is often dwelt on. However, not nearly enough thought is given to what it means, and under what conditions it is possible. Would it not be better if the salutations addressed to the Soviets and the Bolsheviks were *more frequently* accompanied by a *profound analysis* of the reasons why the Bolsheviks have been able to build up the discipline needed by the revolutionary proletariat?

As a current of political thought and as a political party, Bolshevism has existed since 1903. Only the history of Bolshevism during the *entire* period of its existence can satisfactorily explain why it has been able to build up and maintain, under most difficult conditions, the iron discipline needed for the victory of the proletariat.

The first questions to arise are, how is the discipline of the proletariat's revolutionary party maintained? How is it tested? How is it reinforced? First, by the class-consciousness of the proletarian vanguard and by its devotion to the revolution, by its tenacity, self-sacrifice, and heroism. Second, by its ability to link up, maintain the closest contact, and if you wish merge, in certain measure, with the broadest masses of the working people primarily with the proletariat, *but also with the non-proletarian* masses of working people. Third, by the correctness of the political leadership exercised by this vanguard, by the correctness of its political strategy and tactics, provided the broad masses have seen, *from their own experience*, that they are correct. Without these conditions, discipline in a revolutionary party really capable of being the party of the advanced class, whose mission it is to overthrow the bourgeoisie and transform the whole of society, cannot be achieved. Without these conditions, all attempts to establish discipline inevitably fall flat and end up in phrase mongering and clowning. On the other hand, these conditions cannot emerge at once. They are created only by prolonged effort and hard-won experience. Their creation is facilitated by a correct revolutionary theory, which, in its turn, is not a dogma, but assumes final shape only in close connection with the practical activity of a truly mass and truly revolutionary movement.

The fact that, in 1917–20, Bolshevism was able, under unprecedentedly difficult conditions, to build up and successfully maintain the strictest centralization and iron discipline was due simply to a number of historical peculiarities of Russia.

On the one hand, Bolshevism arose in 1903 on a very firm foundation of Marxist theory. The correctness of this revolutionary theory, and of it alone, has been proved, not only by world experience throughout the nineteenth century, but especially by the experience of the seeking's and vacillations, the errors, and disappointments of revolutionary thought in Russia. For about half a century, approximately from the forties to the nineties of the last century progressive thought in Russia, oppressed by a most brutal and reactionary tsarism, sought eagerly for a correct revolutionary theory, and followed with the utmost diligence and thoroughness each and every "last word" in this sphere in Europe and America. Russia achieved Marxism the only correct revolutionary theory through the *agony* she experienced in the course of half a century of unparalleled torment and sacrifice, of unparalleled revolutionary heroism, incredible energy, devoted searching, study, practical trial, disappointment. verification, and comparison with European experience. Thanks to the political emigration caused by tsarism, revolutionary Russia, in the second half of the nineteenth century, acquired a wealth of international links and excellent information on the forms and theories of the world revolutionary movement, such as no other country possessed.

On the other hand, Bolshevism, which had arisen on this granite foundation of theory, went through fifteen years of practical history (1903–17) unequalled anywhere in the world in its wealth of experience. During those fifteen years, no other country knew anything even approximating to that revolutionary experience, that rapid and varied succession of different forms of the movement legal and illegal, peaceful, and stormy, underground, and open local circles and mass movements, and parliamentary and terrorist forms. In no other country has there been concentrated, in so brief a period, such a wealth of forms, shades, and methods of struggle of *all* classes of modern society, a struggle which, owing to the backwardness of the country and the severity of the tsarist yoke, matured with exceptional rapidity, and assimilated most eagerly and successfully the appropriate "last word" of American and European political experience.

The Principal Stages In The History Of Bolshevism

The years of preparation for revolution (1903–05)

The approach of a great storm was sensed everywhere. All classes were in a state of ferment and preparation. Abroad, the press of the political exiles discussed the theoretical aspects of *all* the fundamental problems of the revolution. Representatives of the three main classes, of the three principal political trends, the liberal-bourgeois, the petty-bourgeois-democratic (concealed behind "social-democratic" and "social-revolutionary" labels [2]), and the proletarian-revolutionary anticipated and prepared the impending open class struggle by waging a most bitter struggle on issues of programme and tactics. All the issues on which the masses waged an armed struggle in 1905–07 and 1917–20 can (and should) be studied, in their embryonic form, in the press of the period. Among these three main trends there were, of course, a host of intermediate, transitional, or half-hearted forms. It would be more correct to say that those political and ideological trends which were genuinely of a class nature crystallized in the struggle of press organs, parties, factions, and groups; the classes were forging the requisite political and ideological weapons for the impending battles.

The years of revolution (1905–07). All classes came out into the open. All programmatical and tactical views were tested by the action of the masses. In its extent and acuteness, the strike struggle had no parallel anywhere in the world. The economic strike developed into a political strike, and the latter into insurrection. The relations between the proletariat, as the leader, and the vacillating and unstable peasantry, as the led, were tested in practice. The Soviet form of organization came into being in the spontaneous development of the struggle. The controversies of that period over the significance of the Soviets anticipated the great struggle of 1917–20. The alternation of parliamentary and non-parliamentary forms of struggle, of the tactics of boycotting parliament and that of participating in parliament, of legal and illegal forms of struggle, and likewise their interrelations and connections, all this was marked by an extraordinary wealth of content. As for teaching the fundamentals of political science to masses and leaders, to classes and parties alike, each month of this period was equivalent to an entire year of "peaceful" and "constitutional" development. Without the "dress rehearsal" of 1905, the victory of the October Revolution in 1917 would have been impossible.

The years of reaction (1907–10). Tsarism was victorious. All the revolutionary and opposition parties were smashed. Depression, demoralization, splits, discord, defection, and pornography took the place of politics. There was an ever-greater drift towards philosophical idealism; mysticism became the garb of counter-revolutionary sentiments. At the same time, however, it was this great defeat that taught the revolutionary parties and the revolutionary class a real and very useful lesson, a lesson in historical dialectics, a lesson in an understanding of the political struggle, and in the art and science of waging that struggle. It is at moments of need that one learns who one's friends are. Defeated armies learn their lesson.

Victorious tsarism was compelled to speed up the destruction of the remnants of the pre-bourgeois, patriarchal mode of life in Russia. The country's development along bourgeois lines proceeded apace. Illusions that stood outside and above class distinctions, illusions concerning the possibility of avoiding capitalism, were scattered to the winds. The class struggle manifested itself in a quite new and more distinct way.

The revolutionary parties had to complete their education. They were learning how to attack. Now they had to realize that such knowledge must be supplemented with the knowledge of how to retreat in good order. They had to realize, and it is from bitter experience that the revolutionary class learns to realize this that victory is impossible unless one has learned how to attack and retreat properly. Of all the defeated opposition and revolutionary parties, the Bolsheviks effected the most orderly retreat, with the least loss to their "army", with its core best preserved, with the least significant splits (in point of depth and incurability), with the least demoralization, and in the best condition to resume work on the broadest scale and in the most correct and energetic manner. The Bolsheviks achieved this only because they ruthlessly exposed and expelled the revolutionary phrasemongers, those who did not wish to understand that one had to retreat, that one had to know how to retreat, and that one had absolutely to learn how to work legally in the most reactionary of parliaments, in the most reactionary of trade unions, co-operative and insurance societies and similar organizations.

The years of revival (1910–14). At first progress was incredibly slow, then, following the Lena events of 1912, it became somewhat more rapid. Overcoming unprecedented difficulties, the Bolsheviks thrust back the Mensheviks, whose role as bourgeois agents in the working-class movement was clearly realized by the entire bourgeoisie after 1905, and whom the bourgeoisie therefore supported in a thousand ways against the Bolsheviks. But the Bolsheviks would never have succeeded in doing this had they not followed the correct tactics of combining illegal work with the utilization of "legal opportunities", which they made a point of doing. In the elections to the arch-reactionary Duma, the Bolsheviks won the full support of the worker curia.

The First Imperialist World War (1914–17). Legal parliamentarianism, with an extremely reactionary "parliament", rendered most useful service to the Bolsheviks, the party of the revolutionary proletariat. The Bolshevik deputies were exiled to Siberia. [3] All shades of social-imperialism, social-chauvinism, social-patriotism, inconsistent and consistent internationalism, pacifism, and the revolutionary repudiation of pacifist illusions found full expression in the Russian émigré press. The learned fools and the old women of the Second International, who had arrogantly and contemptuously turned up their noses at the abundance of "factions" in the Russian socialist movement and at the bitter struggle they were waging among themselves, were unable when the war deprived them of their vaunted "legality" in all the advanced countries to organize anything even approximating such a free (illegal) interchange of views and such a free (illegal) evolution of correct views as the Russian revolutionaries did in Switzerland and in a number of other countries. That was why both the avowed social-patriots and the "Kautskyites" of all countries proved to be the worst traitors to the proletariat. One of the principal reasons why Bolshevism was able to achieve victory in 1917–20 was that, since the end of 1914, it has been ruthlessly exposing the baseness and vileness of social-chauvinism and "Kautskyism" (to which Longuetism [4,5] in France, the views of the Fabians [6] and the leaders of the Independent Labour Party [7] in Britain, of Turati in Italy, etc., correspond), the masses later becoming more and more convinced, from their own experience, of the correctness of the Bolshevik views.

The second revolution in Russia (February to October 1917). Tsarism's senility and obsoleteness had (with the aid of the blows and hardships of a most agonizing war) created an incredibly destructive force directed against it. Within a few days Russia was transformed into a democratic bourgeois republic, freer in war conditions than any other country in the world. The leaders of the opposition and revolutionary parties began to set up a government, just as is done in the most "strictly parliamentary" republics; the fact that a man had been a leader of an opposition party in parliament even in a most reactionary parliament *facilitated* his subsequent role in the revolution.

In a few weeks the Mensheviks and Socialist-Revolutionaries thoroughly assimilated all the methods and manners, the arguments and sophistries of the European heroes of the Second International, of the ministerialists [8] and other opportunist riff-raff. Everything we now read about the Scheidemanns and Noskes, about Kautsky and Hilferding, Renner and Austerlitz, Otto Bauer, and Fritz Adler, Turati and Longuet, about the Fabians and the leaders of the Independent Labour Party of Britain all this seems to us (and indeed is) a dreary repetition, a reiteration, of an old and familiar refrain. We have already witnessed all this in the instance of the Mensheviks. As history would have it, the opportunists of a backward country became the forerunners of the opportunists in a number of advanced countries.

If the heroes of the Second International have all gone bankrupt and have disgraced themselves over the question of the significance and role of the Soviets and Soviet rule; if the leaders of the three very important parties which have now left the Second International (namely, the German Independent Social-Democratic Party, [9] the French Longuetists and the British Independent Labour Party) have disgraced themselves and become entangled in this question in a most "telling" fashion; if they have all shown themselves slaves to the prejudices of petty-bourgeois democracy (fully in the spirit of the petty-bourgeois of 1848 who called themselves "Social-Democrats") then we can only say that we have *already* witnessed all this in the instance of the Mensheviks. As history would have it, the Soviets came into being in Russia in 1905 from February to October 1917 they were turned to a false use by the Mensheviks, who went bankrupt because of their inability to understand the role and significance of the Soviets; today the idea of Soviet power has emerged *throughout* the *world* and is spreading among the proletariat of all countries with extraordinary speed. Like our Mensheviks, the old heroes of the Second International are *everywhere* going bankrupt, because they are incapable of understanding the role and significance of the Soviets. Experience has proved that, on certain very important questions of the proletarian revolution, *all* countries will inevitably have to do what Russia has done.

Despite views that are today often to be met with in Europe and America, the Bolsheviks began their victorious struggle against the parliamentary and (in fact) bourgeois republic and against the Mensheviks in a very cautious manner, and the preparations they made for it were by no means simple. At the beginning of the period mentioned, we did not call for the overthrow of the government but explained that it was impossible to overthrow it *without* first changing the composition and the temper of the Soviets. We did *not* proclaim a boycott of the bourgeois parliament, the Constituent Assembly but said and following the April (1917) Conference of our Party began to state officially in the name of the Party that a bourgeois republic with a Constituent Assembly would be better than a bourgeois republic without a Constituent Assembly, but that a "workers' and peasants'" republic, a Soviet republic, would be better than any bourgeois-democratic, parliamentary republic. Without such thorough, circumspect, and long preparations, we could not have achieved victory in October 1917, or have consolidated that victory.

FOOTNOTES

[2] The reference is to the Mensheviks (who formed the Right and opportunist wing of Social-Democracy in the R.S.D.L.P.), and to the Socialist-Revolutionaries.

[3] The reference is to the Bolshevik deputies to the Fourth Duma, namely, A. Y. Badayev, M. K. Muranov, G. I. Petrovsky, F. N. Samoilov, and N. R. Shagov. At the Duma's session of July 26 (August 8), 1914, at which the representatives of all the bourgeois-landowner Duma groups approved tsarist Russia's entry into the imperialist war, the Bolshevik Duma group declared a firm protest; they refused to vote for war credits and launched revolutionary propaganda among the people. In November 1914 the Bolshevik deputies were arrested, in February 1915 they were brought to trial, and exiled for life to Turukhansk Territory in Eastern Siberia. The courageous speeches made by the Bolshevik deputies at their trial, exposing the autocracy, played an important part in anti-war propaganda and in revolutionizing the toiling masses.

[4,5] *Longuetism*, the Centrist trend within the French Socialist Party, headed by Jean Longuet. During the First World War of 1914–18, the Longuetists conducted a policy of conciliation with the social-chauvinists. They rejected the revolutionary struggle and came out for "defence of country" in the imperialist war. Lenin called them petty-bourgeois nationalists. After the victory of the October Socialist Revolution in Russia, the Longuetists called themselves supporters of the proletarian dictatorship, but in fact they remained opposed to it. In December 1920 the Longuetists, together with the avowed reformists, broke away from the Party and joined the so-called Two-and-a-Half International.

[6] *Fabians*, members of the Fabian Society, a British reformist organization founded in 1884. The membership consisted, in the main, of bourgeois intellectuals. The Fabians denied the necessity of the proletariat's class struggle and the socialist revolution and contended that the transition from capitalism to socialism was possible only through petty reforms and the gradual reorganization of society. In 1900 the Fabian Society joined the Labour Party. The Fabians are characterized by Lenin in "British Pacifism and British Dislike of Theory" (see present edition, Vol. 21, pp. 260–65) and elsewhere.

[7] The *Independent Labour* Party of Britain (I.L.P.) a reformist organization founded in 1893 by leaders of the "new trade unions", in conditions of a revival of the strike struggle and the mounting movement for British working-class independence of the bourgeois parties. The I.L.P. included members of the "new trade unions" and those of a number of the old trade unions, as well as intellectuals and petty bourgeoisie who were under the influence of the Fabians. The I.L.P. was headed by James Keir Hardie and Ramsay MacDonald. From its very inception, the I.L.P. took a bourgeois-reformist stand, laying particular stress on parliamentary forms of struggle and parliamentary deals with the Liberals. Lenin wrote of the I.L.P. that "in reality it is an opportunist party always dependent on the bourgeoisie".

[8] *Ministerialism* (or "ministerial socialism", or else Millerandism) the

opportunist tactic of socialists' participation in reactionary bourgeois governments. The term appeared when in 1899, the French socialist Millerand joined the bourgeois government of Waldeck-Rousseau.

[9] The *Independent Social-Democratic Party of Germany, a Centrist party founded in April 1917.*

A split took place at the Congress of the Independent Social-Democratic Party, held in Halle in October 1920, the majority joining the Communist Party of Germany in December 1920. The Right wing formed a separate party, retaining the old name of the Independent Social-Democratic Party. In 1922 the "Independents" re-joined the German Social-Democratic Party.

The Struggle Against Which Enemies Within The Working-Class Movement Helped Bolshevism Develop, Gain Strength, And Become Steeled

First and foremost, the struggle against opportunism which in 1914 definitely developed into social-chauvinism and definitely sided with the bourgeoisie, against the proletariat. Naturally, this was Bolshevism's principal enemy within the working-class movement. It still remains the principal enemy on an international scale. The Bolsheviks have been devoting the greatest attention to this enemy. This aspect of Bolshevik activities is now fairly well known abroad too.

It was, however, different with Bolshevism's other enemy within the working-class movement. Little is known in other countries of the fact that Bolshevism took shape, developed, and became steeled in the long years of struggle against *petty* bourgeois *revolutionism*, which smacks of anarchism, or borrows something from the latter and, in all essential matters, does not measure up to the conditions and requirements of a consistently proletarian class struggle. Marxist theory has established and the experience of all European revolutions and revolutionary movements has fully confirmed that the petty proprietor, the small master (a social type existing on a very extensive and even mass scale in many European countries), who, under capitalism, always suffers oppression and very frequently a most acute and rapid deterioration in his conditions of life, and even ruin, easily goes to revolutionary extremes, but is incapable of perseverance, organization, discipline and steadfastness. A petty bourgeois driven to frenzy by the horrors of capitalism is a social phenomenon which, like anarchism, is characteristic of all capitalist countries. The instability of such revolutionism, its barrenness, and its tendency to turn rapidly into submission, apathy, phantasms, and even a frenzied infatuation with one bourgeois fad or another, all this is common knowledge. However, a theoretical or abstract recognition of these truths does not at all rid revolutionary parties of old errors, which always crop up at unexpected occasions, in somewhat new forms, in hitherto unfamiliar garb or surroundings, in an unusual a more or less unusual situation.

Anarchism was not infrequently a kind of penalty for the opportunist sins of the working-class movement. The two monstrosities complemented each other. And if in Russia despite the more petty-bourgeois composition of her population as compared with the other European countries anarchism's influence was negligible during the two revolutions (of 1905 and 1917) and the preparations for them, this should no doubt stand partly to the credit of Bolshevism, which has always waged a most ruthless and uncompromising struggle against opportunism. I say "partly", since of still greater importance in weakening anarchism's influence in Russia was the circumstance that in the past (the seventies of the nineteenth century) it was able to develop inordinately and to reveal its absolute erroneousness, its unfitness to serve the revolutionary class as a guiding theory.

When it came into being in 1903, Bolshevism took over the tradition of a ruthless struggle against petty-bourgeois, semi-anarchist (or dilettante-anarchist) revolutionism, a tradition which had always existed in revolutionary Social-Democracy and had become particularly strong in our country during the years 1900–03, when the foundations for a mass party of the revolutionary proletariat were being laid in Russia.

Bolshevism took over and carried on the struggle against a party which, more than any other, expressed the tendencies of petty-bourgeois revolutionism, namely, the "Socialist-Revolutionary" Party, and waged that struggle on three main issues. First, that party, which rejected Marxism, stubbornly refused (or it might be more correct to say: was unable) to understand the need for a strictly objective appraisal of the class forces and their alignment, before taking any political action. Second, this party considered itself particularly "revolutionary", or "Left", because of its recognition of individual terrorism, assassination something that we Marxists emphatically rejected. It was, of course, only on grounds of expediency that we rejected individual terrorism, whereas people who were capable of condemning "on principle" the terror of the Great French Revolution, or, in general, the terror employed by a victorious revolutionary party which is besieged by the bourgeoisie of the whole world, were ridiculed and laughed to scorn by Plekhanov in 1900–03, when he was a Marxist and a revolutionary. Third, the "Socialist-Revolutionaries" thought it very "Left" to sneer at the comparatively insignificant opportunist sins of the German Social-Democratic Party, while they themselves imitated the extreme opportunists of that party, for example, on the agrarian question, or on the question of the dictatorship of the proletariat.

History, incidentally, has now confirmed on a vast and world-wide scale the opinion we have always advocated, namely, that German *revolutionary* Social-Democracy (note that as far back as 1900–03 Plekhanov demanded Bernstein's expulsion from the Party, and in 1913 the Bolsheviks, always continuing this tradition, exposed Legien's [10] baseness, vileness and treachery) came closest to being the party the revolutionary proletariat needs in order to achieve victory. Today, in 1920, after all the ignominious failures and crises of the war period and the early post-war years, it can be plainly seen that, of all the Western parties, the German revolutionary Social-Democrats produced the finest leaders and recovered and gained new strength more rapidly than the others did. This may be seen in the instances both of the Spartacists [11] and the Left, proletarian wing of the Independent

Social-Democratic Party of Germany, which is waging an incessant struggle against the opportunism and spinelessness of the Kautskys, Hilferdings, Ledebours and Crispiens. If we now cast a glance to take in a complete historical period, namely, from the Paris Commune to the first Socialist Soviet Republic, we shall find that Marxism's attitude to anarchism in general stands out most definitely and unmistakably. In the final analysis, Marxism proved to be correct, and although the anarchists rightly pointed to the opportunist views on the state prevalent among most of the socialist parties, it must be said, first, that this opportunism was connected with the distortion, and even deliberate suppression, of Marx's views on the state (in my book, The State and Revolution, I pointed out that for thirty-six years, from 1875 to 1911, Bebel withheld a letter by Engels,[12] which very clearly, vividly, bluntly and definitively exposed the opportunism of the current Social-Democratic views on the state); second, that the rectification of these opportunist views, and the recognition of Soviet power and its superiority to bourgeois parliamentary democracy proceeded most rapidly and extensively among those trends in the socialist parties of Europe and America that were most Marxist.

The struggle that Bolshevism waged against "Left" deviations within its own Party assumed particularly large proportions on two occasions: in 1908, on the question of whether or not to participate in a most reactionary "parliament" and in the legal workers' societies, which were being restricted by most reactionary laws; and again in 1918 (the Treaty of Brest-Litovsk [13]), on the question of whether one "compromise" or another was permissible.

In 1908 the "Left" Bolsheviks were expelled from our Party for stubbornly refusing to understand the necessity of participating in a most reactionary "parliament". [14] The "Lefts" among whom there were many splendid revolutionaries who subsequently were (and still are) commendable members of the Communist Party based themselves particularly on the successful experience of the 1905 boycott. When, in August 1905, the tsar proclaimed the convocation of a consultative "parliament", [15] the Bolsheviks called for its boycott, in the teeth of all the opposition parties and the Mensheviks, and the "parliament" was in fact swept away by the revolution of October 1905. [16] The boycott proved correct at the time, not because nonparticipation in reactionary parliaments is correct in general, but because we accurately appraised the objective situation, which was leading to the rapid development of the mass strikes first into a political strike, then into a revolutionary strike, and finally into an uprising. Moreover, the struggle centred at that time on the question of whether the convocation of the first representative assembly should be left to the tsar, or an attempt should be made to wrest its convocation from the old regime. When there was not, and could not be, any certainty that the objective situation was of a similar kind, and when there was no certainty of a similar trend and the same rate of development, the boycott was no longer correct.

The Bolsheviks' boycott of "parliament" in 1905 enriched the revolutionary proletariat with highly valuable political experience and showed that, when legal and illegal parliamentary and non-parliamentary forms of struggle are combined, it is sometimes useful and even essential to reject parliamentary forms. It would, however, be highly erroneous to apply this experience blindly, imitatively, and uncritically to *other* conditions and *other* situations. The Bolsheviks' boycott of the Duma in 1906 was a mistake, although a minor and easily remediable one. [*] The boycott of the Duma in 1907, 1908 and subsequent years was a most serious error and difficult to remedy, because, on the one hand, a very rapid rise of the revolutionary tide and its conversion into an uprising was not to be expected, and, on the other hand, the entire historical situation attendant upon the renovation of the bourgeois monarchy called for legal and illegal activities being combined. Today, when we look back at this fully completed historical period, whose connection with subsequent periods has now become quite clear, it becomes most obvious that in 1908–14 the Bolsheviks could not have preserved (let alone strengthened and developed) the core of the revolutionary party of the proletariat, had they not upheld, in a most strenuous struggle, the viewpoint that it was *obligatory* to combine legal and illegal forms of struggle, and that it was *obligatory* to participate even in a most reactionary parliament and in a number of other institutions hemmed in by reactionary laws (sick benefit societies, etc.).

In 1918 things did not reach a split. At that time the "Left" Communists formed only a separate group or "faction" within our Party, and that not for long. In the same year, 1918, the most prominent representatives of "Left Communism", for example, Comrades Radek and Bukharin, openly acknowledged their error. It had seemed to them that the Treaty of Brest-Litovsk was a compromise with the imperialists, which was inexcusable on principle and harmful to the party of the revolutionary proletariat. It was indeed a compromise with the imperialists, but it was a compromise which, under the circumstances, *had to be made*.

Today, when I hear our tactics in signing the Brest-Litovsk Treaty being attacked by the Socialist-Revolutionaries, for instance, or when I hear Comrade Lansbury say, in a conversation with me, "Our British trade union leaders say that if it was permissible for the Bolsheviks to compromise, it is permissible for them to compromise too", I usually reply by first of all giving a simple and "popular" example:

Imagine that your car is held up by armed bandits. You hand them over your money, passport, revolver, and car. In return you are rid of the pleasant company of the bandits. That is unquestionably a compromise. "Do ut des" (I "give" you money, firearms and a car "so that you give" me the opportunity to get away from you with a whole skin). It would, however, be difficult to find a sane man who would declare such a compromise to be "inadmissible on principle", or who would call the compromiser an accomplice of the bandits (even though the bandits might use the car and the firearms for further robberies). Our compromise with the bandits of German imperialism was just that kind of compromise.

But when, in 1914–18 and then in 1918–20, the Mensheviks and

Socialist-Revolutionaries in Russia, the Scheidemannites (and to a large extent the Kautskyites) in Germany, Otto Bauer and Friedrich Adler (to say nothing of the Renners and Co.) in Austria, the Renaudels and Longuets and Co. in France, the Fabians, the Independents and the Labourites in Britain entered into *compromises* with the bandits of their own bourgeoisie, and sometimes of the "Allied" bourgeoisie, and against the revolutionary proletariat of their own countries, all these gentlemen were actually acting as *accomplices in banditry.*

The conclusion is clear: to reject compromises "on principle", to reject the permissibility of compromises in general, no matter of what kind, is childishness, which it is difficult even to consider seriously. A political leader who desires to be useful to the revolutionary proletariat must be able to distinguish *concrete* cases of compromises that are inexcusable and are an expression of opportunism and *treachery*; he must direct all the force of criticism, the full intensity of merciless exposure and relentless war, against these concrete compromises, and not allow the past masters of "practical" socialism and the parliamentary Jesuits to dodge and wriggle out of responsibility by means of disquisitions on "compromises in general". It is in this way that the "leaders" of the British trade unions, as well as of the Fabian society and the "Independent" Labour Party, dodge responsibility *for the treachery they have perpetrated,* for having made a compromise that is really tantamount to the worst kind of opportunism, treachery, and betrayal.

There are different kinds of compromises. One must be able to analyze the situation and the concrete conditions of each compromise, or of each variety of compromise. One must learn to distinguish between a man who has given up his money and firearms to bandits so as to lessen the evil they can do and to facilitate their capture and execution, and a man who gives his money and firearms to bandits so as to share in the loot. In politics this is by no means always as elementary as it is in this childishly simple example. However, anyone who is out to think up for the workers some kind of recipe that will provide them with cut-and-dried solutions for all contingencies or promises that the policy of the revolutionary proletariat will never come up against difficult or complex situations, is simply a charlatan.

To leave no room for misinterpretation, I shall attempt to outline, if only very briefly, several fundamental rules for the analysis of concrete compromises.

The party which entered into a compromise with the German imperialists by signing the Treaty of Brest-Litovsk had been evolving its internationalism in practice ever since the end of 1914. It was not afraid to call for the defeat of the tsarist monarchy and to condemn "defense of country" in a war between two imperialist robbers. The parliamentary representatives of this party preferred exile in Siberia to taking a road leading to ministerial portfolios in a bourgeois government. The revolution that overthrew tsarism and established a democratic republic put this party to a new and tremendous test, it did not enter into any agreements with its "own" imperialists but prepared and brought about their overthrow. When it had assumed political power, this party did not leave a vestige of either landed or capitalist ownership. After making public and repudiating the imperialists' secret treaties, this party proposed peace to *all* nations, and yielded to the violence of the Brest-Litovsk robbers only after the Anglo-French imperialists had torpedoed the conclusion of a peace, and after the Bolsheviks had done everything humanly possible to hasten the revolution in Germany and other countries. The absolute correctness of this compromise, entered into by such a party in such a situation, is becoming ever clearer and more obvious with every day.

The Mensheviks and the Socialist-Revolutionaries in Russia (like all the leaders of the Second International throughout the world, in 1914–20) began with treachery by directly or indirectly justifying "defense of country", i.e., the defense of their own predatory bourgeoisie. They continued their treachery by entering into a coalition with the bourgeoisie of *their own* country, and fighting, together with *their own* bourgeoisie, against the revolutionary proletariat of their own country. Their bloc, first with Kerensky and the Cadets, and then with Kolchak and Denikin in Russia like the bloc of their *confrères* abroad with the bourgeoisie of *their* respective countries—was in fact desertion to the side of the bourgeoisie, against the proletariat. From beginning to end, their compromise with the bandits of imperialism meant their becoming *accomplices* in imperialist banditry.

FOOTNOTES

[10] Lenin is referring probably to his article "What Should Not Be Copied from the German Labour Movement", published in the Bolshevik magazine *Prosveshcheniye* in April 1914 (see present edition, Vol. 20, pp. 254–58). Here Lenin exposed the treacherous behaviour of Karl Legien, the German Social-Democrat who in 1912, in addressing the Congress of the U.S.A., praised U.S. official circles and bourgeois parties.

[11] *Spartacists*—members of the Spartacus League founded in January 1916, during the First World War, under the leadership of Karl Liebknecht, Rosa Luxemburg, Franz Mehring and Clara Zetkin. The Spartacists conducted revolutionary anti-war propaganda among the masses and exposed the expansionist policy of German imperialism and the treachery of the Social-Democratic leaders. However, the Spartacists, the German Left wing did not get rid of their semi-Menshevik errors on the most important questions of theory and tactics. A criticism of the German Left-wing's mistakes is given in Lenin's works "On Junius's Pamphlet" (see present edition, Vol. 22, pp. 297–305), "A Caricature of Marxism and Imperialist Economism" (see Vol. 23, pp. 28–76) and elsewhere.

In April 1917, the Spartacists joined the Centrist Independent Social-Democratic Party of Germany, preserving their organizational independence. After the November 1918 revolution in Germany, the Spartacists broke away from the "Independents", and in December of the same year founded the Communist Party of Germany.

[12] The reference is to Frederick Engels's letter to August Bebel,

written on March 18–28, 1875.

[13] The Treaty of Brest-Litovsk was signed between Soviet Russia and the powers of the Quadruple Alliance (Germany, Austria-Hungary, Bulgaria and Turkey) on March 3, 1918, at Brest-Litovsk and ratified on March 15 by the Fourth (Extraordinary) All-Russia Congress of Soviets. The peace terms were very harsh for Soviet Russia. According to the treaty, Poland, almost all the Baltic states, and part of Byelorussia were placed under the control of Germany and Austria-Hungary. The Ukraine was separated from Soviet Russia, becoming a state dependent on Germany. Turkey gained control of the cities of Kars, Batum and Ardagan. In August 1918, Germany imposed on Soviet Russia a supplementary treaty and a financial agreement containing new and exorbitant demands.

The treaty prevented further needless loss of life and gave the R.S.F.S.R. the ability to shift its attention to urgent domestic matters. The signing of the Treaty of Brest-Litovsk promoted the struggle for peace among the broad masses of all the warring nations and denounced the war as a struggle between imperialist powers. On November 13, 1918, following the November revolution in Germany, which overthrew the monarchist regime, the All-Russia Central Executive Committee annulled the predatory Treaty of Brest-Litovsk.

[14] The reference is to the otzovists [*the term otzovist derives from the Russian verb "otozvat" meaning "to recall". Ed.*] and ultimatumists, the struggle against whom developed in 1908, and in 1909 resulted in the expulsion of A. Bogdanov, the otzovist leader, from the Bolshevik Party. Behind a screen of revolutionary phrases, the otzovists demanded the recall of the Social-Democrat deputies from the Third Duma and the cessation of activities in legal organisations such as the trade unions, the co-operatives, etc. Ultimatumism was a variety of otzovism. The ultimatumists did not realize the necessity of conducting persistent day by day work with the Social-Democrat deputies, so as to make them consistent revolutionary parliamentarians. They proposed that an ultimatum should be presented to the Social-Democratic group in

the Duma, demanding their absolute subordination to decisions of the Party's Central Committee; should the deputies fail to comply, they were to be recalled from the Duma. A conference of the enlarged editorial board of the Bolshevik paper Proletary, held in June 1909, pointed out in its decision that "Bolshevism, as a definite trend in the R.S.D.L.P., had nothing in common either with otzovism or with ultimatumism". The conference urged the Bolsheviks "to wage a most resolute struggle against these deviations from the path of revolutionary Marxism" (*KPSS v rezolutsiyakh i resheniyakh syezdov, konferentsii i plenumov TsK* (*The C.P.S.U. in the Resolutions and Decisions of Its Congresses, Conferences and Plenums of the Central Committee*), Part I, 1954, p. 221).

[15] On August 6 (19), 1905, the tsar's manifesto was made public, proclaiming the law on the setting up of the Duma and the election procedures. This body was known as the Bulygin Duma, after A.G. Bulygin, the Minister of the Interior, whom the tsar entrusted with drawing up the Duma draft. According to the latter, the Duma had no legislative functions, but could merely discuss certain questions as a consultative body under the tsar. The Bolsheviks called upon the workers and peasants to actively boycott the Bulygin Duma and concentrate all agitation on the slogans of an armed uprising, a revolutionary army, and a provisional revolutionary government. The boycott campaign against the Bulygin Duma was used by the Bolsheviks to mobilise all the revolutionary forces, organize mass political strikes, and prepare for an armed uprising. Elections to the Bulygin Duma were not held and the government was unable to convene it. The Duma was swept away by the mounting tide of the revolution and the all-Russia October political strike of 1905.

[16] Lenin is referring to the *all-Russia October political strike* of 1905, during the first Russian revolution. This strike, which involved over two million people, was conducted under the slogan of the overthrow of the tsarist autocracy, an active boycott of the Bulygin Duma, the summoning of a Constituent Assembly and the establishment of a democratic republic. The all-Russia political strike showed the

strength of the working-class movement, fostered the development of the revolutionary struggle in the countryside, the army, and the navy. The October strike led the proletariat to the December armed uprising. Concerning the October strike, see the article by V. I. Lenin "The All-Russia Political Strike" (present edition, Vol. 9, pp. 392–95).

[*] What applies to individuals also applies with necessary modifications to politics and parties. It is not he who makes no mistakes that is intelligent. There are no such men, nor can there be. It is he whose errors are not very grave and who is able to rectify them easily and quickly that is intelligent.

"Left-Wing" Communism In Germany. The Leaders, The Party, The Class, The Masses

The German Communists we must now speak of call themselves, not "Left-wingers" but, if I am not mistaken, an "opposition on principle". [17] From what follows below it will, however, be seen that they reveal all the symptoms of the "infantile disorder of Leftism".

Published by the "local group in Frankfurt am Main", a pamphlet reflecting the point of view of this opposition and entitled The Split in the Communist Party of Germany (The Spartacus League) sets forth the substance of this opposition's views most saliently, and with the utmost clarity and concision. A few quotations will suffice to acquaint the reader with that substance:

"The Communist Party is the party of the most determined class struggle. . . ."

". . . Politically, the transitional period (between capitalism and socialism) is one of the proletarian dictatorship. . . ."

". . . The question arises: who is to exercise this dictatorship: the Communist Party or the proletarian class? . . . Fundamentally, should we strive for a dictatorship of the Communist Party, or for a dictatorship of the proletarian class? . . ."

(All italics as in the original)

The author of the pamphlet goes on to accuse the Central Committee of the Communist Party of Germany of seeking ways of achieving a coalition with the Independent Social-Democratic Party of Germany, and of raising "the question of recognizing, in principle, all political means" of struggle, including parliamentarianism, with the sole purpose of concealing its actual and main efforts to form a coalition with the Independents. The pamphlet goes on to say:

"The opposition have chosen another road. They are of the opinion that the question of the rule of the Communist Party and of the dictatorship of the Party is merely one of tactics. In any case, rule by the Communist Party is the ultimate form of any party rule. Fundamentally, we must work for the dictatorship of the proletarian class. And all the measures of the Party, its organizations, methods of struggle, strategy and tactics should be directed to that end. Accordingly, all compromise with other parties, all reversion to parliamentary forms of struggle which have become historically and politically obsolete, and any policy of maneuvering and compromise must be emphatically rejected." "Specifically proletarian methods of revolutionary struggle must be strongly emphasized. New forms of organization must be created on the widest basis and with the widest scope in order to enlist the most extensive proletarian circles and strata to take part in the revolutionary struggle under the leadership of the Communist Party. A Workers' Union, based on factory organizations, should be the rallying point for all revolutionary elements. This should unite all workers who follow the slogan: 'Get out of the trade unions!' It is here that the militant proletariat musters its ranks for battle. Recognition of the class struggle, of the Soviet system and of the dictatorship should be sufficient for enrolment. All subsequent political education of the fighting masses and their political orientation in the struggle are the task of the Communist Party, which stands outside the Workers' Union. . . .

". . . Consequently, two Communist parties are now arrayed against each other:

"One is a party of leaders, which is out to organize the revolutionary struggle and to direct it from above, accepting compromises and parliamentarianism so as to create a situation enabling it to join a coalition government exercising a dictatorship.

"The other is a mass party, which expects an upsurge of the revolutionary struggle from below, which knows and applies a single method in this struggle, a method which clearly leads to the goal and rejects all parliamentary and opportunist methods. That single method is the unconditional overthrow of the bourgeoisie, so as then to set up the proletarian class dictatorship for the accomplishment of socialism. . . .

". . . There, the dictatorship of leaders here the dictatorship of the masses! That is our slogan."

Such are the main features characterizing the views of the opposition in the German Communist Party.

Any Bolshevik who has consciously participated in the development of Bolshevism since 1903 or has closely observed that development will at once say, after reading these arguments, "What old and familiar rubbish! What 'Left-wing' childishness!"

But let us examine these arguments a little more closely.

The mere presentation of the question, "dictatorship of the party or dictatorship of the class; dictatorship (party) of the leaders, or dictatorship (party) of the masses?" testifies to most incredibly and hopelessly muddled thinking. These people want to invent something quite out of the ordinary, and, in their effort to be clever, make themselves ridiculous. It is common knowledge that the masses are divided into classes, that the masses can be contrasted with classes only by contrasting the vast majority in general, regardless of division according to status in the social system of production, with categories holding a definite status in the social system of production; that as a rule and in most cases at least in present-day civilized countries classes are led by political parties; that political parties, as a general rule, are run by more or less stable groups composed of the most authoritative, influential and experienced members, who are elected to the most responsible positions, and are called leaders. All this is elementary. All this is clear and simple. Why replace this with some kind of rigmarole, some new Volapük? On the one hand, these people seem to have got muddled when they found themselves in a predicament, when the party's abrupt transition from legality to illegality upset the customary, normal, and simple relations between leaders, parties, and classes. In Germany, as in other European countries, people had become too accustomed to legality, to the free and proper election of "leaders" at regular party congresses, to the convenient method of testing the class composition of parties through parliamentary elections, mass meetings the press, the sentiments of the trade unions and other associations, etc. When, instead of this customary procedure, it became necessary, because of the stormy development of the revolution and the development of the civil war, to go over rapidly from legality to illegality, to combine the two, and to adopt the "inconvenient" and "undemocratic" methods of selecting, or forming, or preserving "groups of leaders" people lost their bearings and began to think up some unmitigated nonsense. Certain members of the Communist Party of Holland, who were unlucky enough to be born in a small country with traditions and conditions of highly privileged and highly stable legality, and who had never seen a transition from legality to illegality, probably fell into confusion, lost their heads, and helped create these absurd inventions.

On the other hand, one can see simply a thoughtless and incoherent use of the now "fashionable" terms: "masses" and "leaders". These people have heard and memorized a great many attacks on "leaders", in which the latter have been contrasted with the "masses"; however, they have proved unable to think matters out and gain a clear understanding of what it was all about.

The divergence between "leaders" and "masses" was brought

out with particular clarity and sharpness in all countries at the end of the imperialist war and following it. The principal reason for this was explained many times by Marx and Engels between the years 1852 and 1892, from the example of Britain. That country's exclusive position led to the emergence, from the "masses", of a semi petty bourgeois, opportunist "labour aristocracy". The leaders of this labour aristocracy were constantly going over to the bourgeoisie and were directly or indirectly on its pay roll. Marx earned the honour of incurring the hatred of these disreputable persons by openly branding them as traitors. Present-day (twentieth century) imperialism has given a few advanced countries an exceptionally privileged position, which, everywhere in the Second International, has produced a certain type of traitor, opportunist, and social-chauvinist leaders, who champion the interests of their own craft, their own section of the labour aristocracy. The opportunist parties have become separated from the "masses", i.e., from the broadest strata of the working people, their majority, the lowest-paid workers. The revolutionary proletariat cannot be victorious unless this evil is combated, unless the opportunist, social-traitor leaders are exposed, discredited, and expelled. That is the policy the Third International has embarked on.

To go so far, in this connection, as to contrast, in general, the dictatorship of the masses with a dictatorship of the leaders is ridiculously absurd, and stupid. What is particularly amusing is that, in fact, instead of the old leaders, who hold generally accepted views on simple matters, new leaders are brought forth (under cover of the slogan "Down with the leaders!"), who talk rank stuff and nonsense. Such are Laufenberg, Wolffheim, Horner [18], Karl Schroder, Friedrich Wendel and Karl Erler, [*2] in Germany. Erler's attempts to give the question more "profundity" and to proclaim that in general political parties are unnecessary and "bourgeois" are so supremely absurd that one can only shrug one's shoulders. It all goes to drive home the truth that a minor error can always assume monstrous proportions if it is persisted in, if profound justifications are sought for it, and if it is carried to its logical conclusion.

Repudiation of the Party principle and of Party discipline that is what the opposition has arrived at. And this is tantamount to completely disarming the proletariat in the interests of the bourgeoisie. It all adds up to that petty-bourgeois diffuseness and instability, that incapacity for sustained effort, unity, and organized action, which, if encouraged, must inevitably destroy any proletarian revolutionary movement. From the standpoint of communism, repudiation of the Party principle means attempting to leap from the eve of capitalism's collapse (in Germany), not to the lower or the intermediate phase of communism, but to the higher. We in Russia (in the third year since the overthrow of the bourgeoisie) are making the first steps in the transition from capitalism to socialism or the lower stage of communism. Classes still remain and will remain everywhere for years after the proletariat's conquest of power. Perhaps in Britain, where there is no peasantry (but where petty proprietors exist), this period may be shorter. The abolition of classes means, not merely ousting the landowners and the capitalists that is something we accomplished with comparative ease; it also means abolishing the small commodity producers, and they cannot be ousted, or crushed; we must learn to live with them. They can (and must) be transformed and re-educated only by means of very prolonged, slow, and cautious organizational work. They surround the proletariat on every side with a petty-bourgeois atmosphere, which permeates and corrupts the proletariat, and constantly causes among the proletariat relapses into petty-bourgeois spinelessness, disunity, individualism, and alternating moods of exaltation and dejection. The strictest centralization and discipline are required within the political party of the proletariat in order to counteract this, in order that the organizational role of the proletariat (and that is its principal role) may be exercised correctly, successfully, and victoriously. The dictatorship of the proletariat means a persistent struggle bloody and bloodless, violent, and peaceful, military, and economic, educational, and administrative against the forces and traditions of the old society. The force of habit in millions and tens of millions is a most formidable force. Without a party of iron that has been tempered in the struggle, a party enjoying the confidence of all honest people in the class in question, a party capable of watching and influencing the mood of the masses, such a struggle cannot be waged successfully. It is a thousand times easier to vanquish the centralized big bourgeoisie than to "vanquish" the millions upon millions of petty proprietors; however, through their ordinary, everyday, imperceptible, elusive, and demoralizing activities, they produce the very results which the bourgeoisie need, and which tend to restore the bourgeoisie. Whoever brings about even the slightest weakening of the iron discipline of the party of the proletariat (especially during its dictatorship), is actually aiding the bourgeoisie against the proletariat.

Parallel with the question of the leaders the party, the class, the masses, we must pose the question of the "reactionary" trade unions. But first I shall take the liberty of making a few concluding remarks based on the experience of our Party. There have always been attacks on the "dictatorship of leaders" in our Party. The first time I heard such attacks, I recall, was in 1895, when, officially, no party yet existed, but a central group was taking shape in St. Petersburg, which was to assume the leadership of the district groups. [20] At the Ninth Congress of our Party (April 1920) [21], there was a small opposition, which also spoke against the "dictatorship of leaders", against the "oligarchy", and so on. There is therefore nothing surprising, new, or terrible in the "infantile disorder" of "Left-wing communism" among the Germans. The ailment involves no danger, and after it the organism even becomes more robust. In our case, on the other hand, the rapid alternation of legal and illegal work, which made it necessary to keep the general staff, the leaders under cover and cloak them in the greatest secrecy, sometimes gave rise to extremely dangerous consequences. The worst of these was that in 1912 the agent provocateur Malinovsky got into the Bolshevik Central Committee. He betrayed scores and scores of the best and most loyal comrades, caused them to be sentenced to penal servitude, and hastened the death of many of them. That he did not cause still greater harm was due to the correct balance between legal and illegal work. As member of the Party's Central Committee and Duma deputy, Malinovsky was forced, in order to gain our confidence, to help us establish legal daily papers, which even under tsarism were able to wage a struggle against the Menshevik opportunism and to spread the fundamentals of Bolshevism in a suitably disguised form. While, with one hand, Malinovsky sent scores and scores of the finest Bolsheviks to penal servitude and death, he was obliged, with the other, to assist in the education of scores and scores of thousands of new Bolsheviks through the medium of the legal press. Those German (and also British, American, French, and Italian) comrades who are faced with the task of learning how to conduct revolutionary work within the reactionary trade unions would do well to give serious thought to this fact. [*3]

In many countries, including the most advanced, the bourgeoisie are undoubtedly sending agents *provocateurs* into the Communist parties and will continue to do so. A skillful combining of illegal and legal work is one of the ways to combat this danger.

FOOTNOTES

[17] The "opposition on principle", a group of German Left-wing Communists advocating anarcho-syndicalist views. When the Second Congress of the Communist Party of Germany, which was held in Heidelberg in October 1919, expelled the opposition, the latter formed the so-called Communist Workers' Party of Germany, in April 1920. To facilitate the unification of all German communist forces and win over the finest proletarian. elements in the C.W.P.G., the opposition was temporarily admitted into the Communist International in November 1920 with the rights of a sympathizing member.

However, the Executive Committee of the Communist International still considered the United Communist Party of Germany to be the only authoritative section of the Comin tern. C.W.P.G.'s representatives were admitted into the Comin tern on the condition that they merged with the United Communist Party of Germany and supported all its activities. The C.W.P.G. leaders, however, failed to observe these conditions. The Third Congress of the Communist International, which was held in June–July 1921, and wanted solidarity with workers who still followed the C.W.P.G. leaders, resolved to give the C.W.P.G. two months to call a congress and settle the question of affiliation. The C.W.P.G. Leaders did not obey the Third Congress's resolution and thus placed themselves outside the Communist International. Later the C.W.P.G. degenerated into a small sectarian group without any support in the working class.

[18] Horner, Karl—Anton Pannekoek.

[19] Kommunistische Arbeiterzeitung (The Communist Workers' Newspaper) organ of the anarcho-syndicalist group of the German Leftwing Communists (see Note 17). The newspaper was published in Hamburg from 1919 till 1927. Karl Erler, who is mentioned by V. I. Lenin, was Heinrich Laufenberg's penname.

[20] The reference is to the League of Struggle for the Emancipation of the Working Class organized by V. I. Lenin in the autumn of 1895. The League of Struggle united about twenty Marxist circles in St. Petersburg. It was headed by the Central Group including V. I. Lenin, A. A. Vaneyev, P. K. Zaporozhets, G. M. Krzhizhanovsky, N. K. Krupskaya, L. Martov, M. A. Silvin, V. V. Starkov, and others; five members headed by V. I. Lenin directed the League's activities. The organization was divided into district groups. Progressive workers such as I. V. Babushkin, V. A. Shelgunov and others linked these groups with the factories.

The St. Petersburg League of Struggle for the Emancipation of the Working Class was, in V. I. Lenin's words, the embryo of a revolutionary party based on the working-class movement and giving leadership to the class struggle of the proletariat.

[21] The Congress was held in Moscow from March 29 to April 5, 1920. The Ninth Congress was more numerous than any previous Party congresses. It was attended by 715 delegates, 553 of them with full votes, and 162 with deliberative votes representing a membership of 611,978. Represented were the Party organizations

of Central Russia, the Ukraine, the Urals, Siberia, and other regions recently liberated by the Red Army. Many of the delegates came to the Congress straight from the front.

The agenda of the Congress was as follows:

1. The report of the Central Committee.
2. The immediate tasks of economic construction.
3. The trade union movement.
4. Organizational questions.
5. The tasks of the Communist International.
6. The attitude towards the co-operatives.
7. The change-over to the militia system.
8. Elections to the Central Committee.
9. Miscellaneous.

The Congress was held under the guidance of V. I. Lenin, who was the main speaker on the political work of the Central Committee and replied to the debate on the report. He also spoke on economic construction and co-operation, made the speech at the closing of the Congress, and submitted a proposal on the list of candidates to the Party's Central Committee.

In the resolution "The Immediate Tasks of Economic Development" the Congress noted that "the basic condition of economic rehabilitation of the country is a steady implementation of the single economic plan for the coming historical epoch" (*KPSS v rezolutsiyakh i resheniyakh syezdov, konferentsii i plenumov TsK (The C.P.S.U. in the Resolutions and Decisions of Its Congresses, Conferences and Plenums of the Central Committee*), Part I, 1954, p. 478). The kingpin of the single economic plan was electrification, which V. I. Lenin considered a great programme for a period of 10 to 20 years. The directives of the Ninth Congress were the basis of the plan conclusively drawn up by the State Commission for the Electrification of Russia (the GOELRO plan) and approved by the All-Russia Congress of Soviets in December 1920.

The Congress paid particular attention to the organization of industrial management. The resolution on this question called for the establishment of competent, firm, and energetic one-man management. Taking its guidance from Lenin, the Congress especially stressed the necessity to extensively enlist old and experienced experts.

The anti-Party group of Democratic Centralists, consisting of Sapronov, Osinsky, V. Smirnov and others, came out against the Party line. Behind a cover of phrases about Democratic Centralism but in fact distorting that principle, they denied the need for one-man management at factories, came out against strict Party and state discipline, and alleged that the Central Committee did not give effect to the principle of collective leadership.

The group of Democratic Centralists was supported at the Congress by Rykov, Tomsky, Milyutin and Lomov. The Congress rebuffed the Democratic Centralists and rejected their proposals.

The Congress gave special attention to labour emulation and communist *Subbotniks*. To stimulate such emulation, the extensive application of the bonus system of wages was recommended. The Congress resolved that May 1, the international proletarian holiday, which in 1920 fell on Saturday, should be a mass *Subbotnik* organised throughout Russia.

An important place in the work of the Congress was held by the question of trade unions, which was considered from the viewpoint of adapting the entire work of the trade unions to the accomplishment of the economic tasks. In a resolution on this question, the Congress distinctly defined the trade unions' role, their relations with the state and the Party, forms, and methods of guidance of trade unions by the

Communist Party, as well as forms of their participation in communist construction. The Congress decisively rebuffed the anarcho-syndicalist elements (Shlyapnikov, Lozovsky, Tomsky and Lutovinov), who advocated the "independence" of the trade unions and contraposed them to the Communist Party and the Soviet government.

At a closed meeting held on April 4, the Congress elected a new Central Committee of 19 members and 12 candidate members. The former included V.I. Lenin, A. A. Andreyev, F. E. Dzerzhinsky, M. I. Kalinin, Y. E. Rudzutak, F. A. Sergeyev (Artyom), and J. V. Stalin. On April 5 the Congress concluded its work.

[*2] Karl Erler, "The Dissolution of the Party", *Kommunistische Arbeiterzeitung*, [19] Hamburg, February 7, 1920, No. 32:

> "The working class cannot destroy the bourgeois state without destroying bourgeois democracy, and it cannot destroy bourgeois democracy without destroying parties."

The more muddle-headed of the syndicalists and anarchists in the Latin countries may derive "satisfaction" from the fact that solid Germans, who evidently consider themselves Marxists (by their articles in the above-mentioned paper K. Erler and K. Horner have shown most plainly that they consider themselves sound Marxists but talk incredible nonsense in a most ridiculous manner and reveal their failure to understand the ABC of Marxism), go to the length of making utterly inept statements. Mere acceptance of Marxism does not save one from errors. We Russians know this especially well, because Marxism has been very often the "fashion" in our country.

[*3] Malinovsky was a prisoner of war in Germany. On his return to Russia when the Bolsheviks were in power, he was instantly put on trial and shot by our workers. The Mensheviks attacked us most bitterly for our mistake the fact that an *agent provocateur* had become a member of the Central Committee of our Party. But when, under Kerensky, we demanded the arrest and trial of Rodzyanko, the Chairman of the Duma, because he had known, even before the war, that Malinovsky

was an *agent provocateur and had not informed* the Trudoviks and the workers in the Duma, neither the Mensheviks nor the Socialist-Revolutionaries in the Kerensky government supported our demand, and Rodzyanko remained at large and made off unhindered to join Denikin.

Should Revolutionaries Work In Reactionary Trade Unions?

The German "Lefts" consider that, as far as they are concerned, the reply to this question is an unqualified negative. In their opinion, declamations, and angry outcries (such as uttered by K. Horner in a particularly "solid" and particularly stupid manner) against "reactionary" and "counter-revolutionary" trade unions are sufficient "proof" that it is unnecessary and even inexcusable for revolutionaries and Communists to work in yellow, social-chauvinist, compromising and counter-revolutionary trade unions of the Legien type.

However firmly the German "Lefts" may be convinced of the revolutionism of such tactics, the latter are in fact fundamentally wrong, and contain nothing but empty phrases.

To make this clear, I shall begin with our own experience, in keeping with the general plan of the present pamphlet, which is aimed at applying to Western Europe whatever is universally practicable, significant, and relevant in the history and the present-day tactics of Bolshevism.

In Russia today, the connection between leaders, party, class, and masses, as well as the attitude of the dictatorship of the proletariat and its party to the trade unions, are concretely as follows: the dictatorship is exercised by the proletariat organized in the Soviets; the proletariat is guided by the Communist Party of Bolsheviks, which, according to the figures of the latest Party Congress (April 1920), has a membership of 611,000. The membership varied greatly both before and after the October Revolution, and used to be much smaller, even in 1918 and 1919.[22] We are apprehensive of an excessive growth of the Party, because careerists and charlatans, who deserve only to be shot, inevitably do all they can to insinuate themselves into the ranks of the ruling party. The last time we opened wide the doors of the Party to workers and peasants only was when (in the winter of 1919) Yudenich was within a few versts of Petrograd, and Denikin was in Orel (about 350 versts from Moscow), i.e., when the Soviet Republic was in mortal danger, and when adventurers, careerists, charlatans and unreliable persons generally could not possibly count on making a profitable career (and had more reason to expect the gallows and torture) by joining the Communists.[23] The Party, which holds annual congresses (the most recent on the basis of one delegate per 1,000 members), is directed by a Central Committee of nineteen elected at the Congress, while the current work in Moscow has to be carried on by still smaller bodies, known as the Organizing Bureau and the Political Bureau, which are elected at plenary meetings of the Central Committee, five members of the Central Committee to each bureau. This, it would appear, is a full-fledged "oligarchy". No important political or organizational question is decided by any state institution in our republic without the guidance of the Party's Central Committee.

In its work, the Party relies directly on the *trade unions*, which, according to the data of the last congress (April 1920), now have a membership of over four million and are formally *non-Party*. Actually, all the directing bodies of the vast majority of the unions, and primarily, of course, of the all-Russia general trade union Centre or bureau (the All-Russia Central Council of Trade Unions), are made up of Communists and carry out all the directives of the Party. Thus, on the whole, we have a formally non-communist, flexible, and relatively wide and very powerful proletarian apparatus, by means of which the Party is closely linked up with the *class* and the *masses*, and by means of which, under the leadership of the Party, the *class dictatorship* is exercised. Without close contacts with the trade unions, and without their energetic support and devoted efforts, not only in economic, *but also in military* affairs, it would of course have been impossible for us to govern the country and to maintain the dictatorship for two and a half months, let alone two and a half years. In practice, these very close contacts naturally call for highly complex and diversified work in the form of propaganda, agitation, timely and frequent conferences, not only with the leading trade union workers, but with influential trade union workers generally; they call for a determined struggle against the Mensheviks, who still have a certain though very small following to whom they teach all kinds of counter-revolutionary machinations, ranging from an ideological defence of (*bourgeois*) democracy and the preaching that the trade unions should be "independent" (independent of proletarian state power!) to sabotage of proletarian discipline, etc., etc.

We consider that contacts with the "masses" through the trade unions are not enough. In the course of our revolution, practical activities have given rise to such institutions as *non-Party workers'* and *peasants' conferences*, and we strive by every means to support, develop, and extend this institution in order to be able to observe the temper of the masses, come closer to them, meet their requirements, promote the best among them to state posts, etc. Under a recent decree on the transformation of the People's Commissariat of State Control into the Workers' and Peasants' Inspection, non-Party conferences of this kind have been empowered to select members of the State Control to carry out various kinds of investigations, etc.

Then, of course, all the work of the Party is carried on through the Soviets, which embrace the working masses irrespective of occupation. The district congresses of Soviets are *democratic* institutions, the like of which even the best of the democratic republics of the bourgeois world have never known; through these congresses (whose proceedings the Party endeavours to follow with the closest attention), as well as by continually appointing class-conscious workers to various posts in the rural districts, the proletariat exercises its role of leader of the peasantry, gives effect to the dictatorship of the urban proletariat wages a systematic struggle against the rich, bourgeois, exploiting and profiteering peasantry, etc.

Such is the general mechanism of the proletarian state power viewed "from above", from the standpoint of the practical implementation of the dictatorship. We hope that the reader will understand why the Russian Bolshevik who has known this mechanism for twenty-five years and has seen it develop out of small, illegal, and underground circles, cannot help regarding all this talk about "from above" or "from below", about the dictatorship of leaders or the dictatorship of the masses, etc., as ridiculous and childish nonsense, something like discussing whether a man's left leg or right arm is of greater use to him.

We cannot but regard as equally ridiculous and childish nonsense the pompous, very learned, and frightfully revolutionary disquisitions of the German Lefts to the effect that Communists cannot and should not work in reactionary trade unions, that it is permissible to turn down such work, that it is necessary to withdraw from the trade unions and create a brand-new and immaculate "Workers' Union" invented by very pleasant (and, probably, for the most part very youthful) Communists, etc., etc.

Capitalism inevitably leaves socialism the legacy, on the one hand, of the old trade and craft distinctions among the workers, distinctions evolved in the course of centuries; on the other hand, trade unions, which only very slowly, in the course of years and years, can and will develop into broader industrial unions with less of the craft union about them (embracing entire industries, and not only crafts, trades and occupations), and later proceed, through these industrial unions, to eliminate the division of labour among people, to educate and school people, give them *all-round development and an all-round training*, so that they are able to do everything. Communism is advancing and must advance towards that goal, and *will* reach it, but only after very many years. To attempt in practice, today, to anticipate this future result of a fully developed, fully stabilized and constituted, fully comprehensive and mature communism would be like trying to teach higher mathematics to a child of four.

We can (and must) begin to build socialism, not with abstract human material, or with human material specially prepared by us, but with the human material bequeathed to us by capitalism. True, that is no easy matter, but no other approach to this task is serious enough to warrant discussion.

The trade unions were a tremendous step forward for the working class in the early days of capitalist development, inasmuch as they marked a transition from the workers' disunity and helplessness to the *rudiments* of class organization. When the *revolutionary party of the proletariat, the highest* form of proletarian class organization, began to take shape (and the Party will not merit the name until it learns to weld the leaders into one indivisible whole with the class and the masses) the trade unions inevitably began to reveal *certain* reactionary features, a certain craft narrow-mindedness, a certain tendency to be non-political, a certain inertness, etc. However, the development of the proletariat did not, and could not, proceed anywhere in the world otherwise than through the trade unions, through reciprocal action between them and the party of the working class. The proletariat's conquest of political power is a gigantic step forward for the proletariat as a class, and the Party must more than ever and in a new way, not only in the old, educate and guide the trade unions, at the same time bearing in mind that they are and will long remain an indispensable "school of communism" and a preparatory school that trains proletarians to exercise their dictatorship, an indispensable organization of the workers for the gradual transfer of the management of the whole economic life of the country to the working *class* (and not to the separate trades), and later to all the working people.

In the sense mentioned above, a *certain* "reactionism" in the trade unions is *inevitable* under the dictatorship of the proletariat. Not to understand this means a complete failure to understand the fundamental conditions of the *transition* from capitalism to socialism. It would be egregious folly to fear *this* "reactionism" or to try to evade or leap over it, for it would mean fearing that function of the proletarian vanguard which consists in training, educating, enlightening, and drawing into the new life the most backward strata and masses of the working class and the peasantry. On the other hand, it would be a still graver error to postpone the achievement of the dictatorship of the proletariat until a time when there will not be a single worker with a narrow-minded craft outlook, or with craft and craft-union prejudices. The art of politics (and the Communist's correct understanding of his tasks) consists in correctly gauging the conditions and the moment when the vanguard of the proletariat can successfully assume power, when it is able during and after the seizure of power to win adequate support from sufficiently broad strata of the working class and of the non-proletarian working masses, and when it is able thereafter to maintain, consolidate and extend its rule by educating, training and attracting ever broader masses of the working people.

Further. In countries more advanced than Russia, a certain reactionism in the trade unions has been and was bound to be manifested in a far greater measure than in our country. Our Mensheviks found support in the trade unions (and to some extents still do so in a small number of unions), as a result of the latter's craft narrow-mindedness, craft selfishness and opportunism. The Mensheviks of the West have acquired a much firmer footing in the trade unions; there the *craft-union, narrow-minded, selfish, case-hardened, covetous, and petty-bourgeois "labour aristocracy", imperialist-minded, and imperialist-corrupted,* has developed into a much stronger section than in our country. That is incontestable. The struggle against the Gomperses, and against the Jouhaux, Hendersons, Merrheims, Legiens and Co. in Western Europe is much more difficult than the struggle against our Mensheviks, who are an *absolutely homogeneous* social and political type. This struggle must be waged ruthlessly, and it must unfailingly be brought as we brought it to a point when all the incorrigible leaders of opportunism and social chauvinism are completely discredited and driven out of the trade unions. Political power cannot be captured (and the attempt to capture it should not be made) until the struggle has reached a *certain* stage. This "certain stage" will be different in different countries and in *different* circumstances; it can be correctly gauged only by thoughtful, experienced, and knowledgeable political leaders of the proletariat in each particular country. (In Russia the elections to the Constituent Assembly in November 1917, a few days after the proletarian revolution of October 25, 1917, were one of the criteria of the success of this struggle. In these elections the Mensheviks were utterly defeated; they received 700,000 votes—1,400,000 if the vote in Transcaucasia is added as against 9,000,000 votes polled by the Bolsheviks. See my article, "The Constituent Assembly Elections and the Dictatorship of the Proletariat",[24] in the *Communist International*[25] No. 7–8.)

We are waging a struggle against the "labour aristocracy" in the name of the masses of the workers and in order to win them over to our side; we are waging the struggle against the opportunist and social-chauvinist leaders in order to win the working class over to our side. It would be absurd to forget this most elementary and most self-evident truth. Yet it is this very absurdity that the German "Left" Communists perpetrate when, *because* of the reactionary and counter-revolutionary character of the trade union top *leadership*, they jump to the conclusion that . . . we must withdraw from the trade unions, refuse to work in them, and create new and *artificial* forms of labour organization! This is so unpardonable a blunder that it is tantamount to the greatest service Communists could render the bourgeoisie. Like all the opportunist, social-chauvinist, and Kautskyite trade union leaders, our Mensheviks are nothing but "agents of the bourgeoisie in the working-class movement" (as we have always said the Mensheviks are), or "labour lieutenants of the capitalist class", to use the splendid and profoundly true expression of the followers of Daniel De Leon in America. To refuse to work in the reactionary trade unions means leaving the insufficiently developed or backward masses of workers under the influence of the reactionary leaders, the agents of the bourgeoisie, the labour aristocrats, or "workers who have become completely bourgeois" (cf. Engels's letter to Marx in 1858 about the British workers[26]).

This ridiculous "theory" that Communists should not work in reactionary trade unions reveals with the utmost clarity the frivolous attitude of the "Left" Communists towards the question of influencing the "masses", and their misuse of clamour about the "masses". If you want to help the "masses" and win the sympathy and support of the "masses", you should not fear difficulties, or pinpricks, chicanery, insults, and persecution from the "leaders" (who, being opportunists and social chauvinists, are in most cases directly or indirectly connected with the bourgeoisie and the police) but must absolutely *work wherever the masses are to be found*. You must be capable of any sacrifice, of overcoming the greatest obstacles, in order to carry on agitation and propaganda systematically, perseveringly, persistently, and patiently in those institutions, societies and associations even the most reactionary in which proletarian or semi-proletarian masses are to be found. The trade unions and the workers' co-operatives (the latter sometimes, at least) are the very organizations in which the masses are to be found. According to figures quoted in the Swedish paper Folkets Dagblad Politiken of March 10, 1920, the trade union membership in Great Britain increased from 5,500,000 at the end of 1917 to 6,600,000 at the end of 1918, an increase of 19 per cent. Towards the close of 1919, the membership was estimated at 7,500,000. I have not got the corresponding figures for France and Germany to hand, but absolutely incontestable and generally known facts testify to a rapid rise in the trade union membership in these countries too.

These facts make crystal clear something that is confirmed by thousands of other symptoms, namely, that class-consciousness and the desire for organization are growing among the proletarian masses, among the rank and file, among the backward elements. Millions of workers in Great Britain, France and Germany are *for the first time* passing from a complete lack of organization to the elementary, lowest, simplest, and (to those still thoroughly imbued with bourgeois-democratic prejudices) most easily comprehensible form of organization, namely, the trade unions; yet the revolutionary but imprudent Left Communists stand by, crying out "the masses", "the masses!" *but refusing to work within the trade unions*, on the pretext that they are "reactionary", and invent a brand-new, immaculate little "Workers' Union", which is guiltless of bourgeois-democratic prejudices and innocent of craft or narrow-minded craft-union sins, a union which, they claim, will be (!) a broad organization. "Recognition of the Soviet system and the dictatorship" will be the *only* (!) condition of membership. (See the passage quoted above.)

It would be hard to imagine any greater ineptitude or greater harm to the revolution than that caused by the "Left" revolutionaries! Why, if we in Russia today, after two and a half years of unprecedented victories over the bourgeoisie of Russia and the Entente, were to make "recognition of the dictatorship" a condition of trade union membership, we would be doing a very foolish thing, damaging our influence among the masses, and helping the Mensheviks. The task devolving on Communists is to *convince* the backward elements, to work *among* them, and not to *fence themselves* off from them with artificial and childishly "Left" slogans.

There can be no doubt that the Gomperses, the Hendersons, the Jonhaux and the Legiens are very grateful to those "Left" revolutionaries who, like the German opposition "on principle" (heaven preserve us from such "principles"!), or like some of the revolutionaries in the American Industrial Workers of the World[27] advocate quitting the reactionary trade unions and refusing to work in them. These men, the "leaders" of opportunism, will no doubt resort to every device of bourgeois diplomacy and to the aid of bourgeois governments, the clergy, the police, and the courts, to keep Communists out of the trade unions, oust them by every means, make their work in the trade unions as unpleasant as possible, and insult, bait and persecute them. We must be able to stand up to all this, agree to make any sacrifice, and even, if need be, to resort to various stratagems, artifices, and illegal methods, to evasions and subterfuges, as long as we get into the trade unions, remain in them, and carryon communist work within them at all costs. Under tsarism we had no "legal opportunities" whatsoever until 1905. However, when Zubatov, agent of the secret police, organised Black-Hundred workers' assemblies, and workingmen's societies for the purpose of trapping revolutionaries and combating them, we sent members of our Party to these assemblies and into these societies (I personally remember one of them, Comrade Babushkin, a leading St. Petersburg factory worker, shot by order of the tsar's generals in 1906). They established contacts with the masses, were able to carry on their agitation, and succeeded in wresting workers from the influence of Zubatov's agents. [*4] Of course, in Western Europe, which is imbued with most deep-rooted legalistic, constitutionalist and bourgeois-democratic prejudices, this is more difficult of achievement. However, it can and must be carried out, and systematically at that.

The Executive Committee of the Third International must, in my opinion, positively condemn, and call upon the next congress of the Communist International to condemn both the policy of refusing to work in reactionary trade unions in general (explaining in detail why such refusal is unwise, and what extreme harm it does to the cause of the proletarian revolution) and, in particular, the line of conduct of some members of the Communist Party of Holland, who whether directly or indirectly, overtly or covertly, wholly or partly, it does not matter have supported this erroneous policy. The Third International must break with the tactics of the Second International, it must not evade or play down points at issue but must pose them in a straightforward fashion. The whole truth has been put squarely to the "Independents"; the whole truth must likewise be put squarely to the "Left" Communists.

FOOTNOTES

[22] Between the February 1917 Revolution and 1919 inclusively, the Party's membership changed as follows: by the Seventh All-Russia Conference of the R.S.D.L.P.(B.) (April 1917) the Party numbered 80,000 members, by the Sixth R.S.D.L.P.(B.) Congress in July–August

1917 about 240,000, by the Seventh Congress of the R.C.P.(B.) in March 1918 not less than 270,000 by the Eighth Congress of the R.C.P.(B.) in March 1919—313,766 members.

[23] The reference is to *Party Week*, which was held in accordance with the resolution of the Eighth Congress of the R.C.P.(B.) on building up the Party's membership. The Party Week was conducted in conditions of the bitter struggle waged by the Soviet state against the foreign intervention and domestic counterrevolution. Party Week was first held in the Petrograd organization of the R.C.P.(B.), August 10–17, 1919 (the second Party Week was held in Petrograd in October–November 1919); between September 20 and 28 a Party Week was held in the Moscow Gubernia organization. Summarizing the experience of the first Party Weeks, the Plenum of the Central Committee of the R.C.P.(B.), held on September 26, 1919, resolved that Party Weeks should be held in cities, the countryside, and the army. At the end of September, the Central Committee addressed a circular to all Party organizations pointing out that, as the re-registration and purge of the membership had been accomplished in almost all-Party organizations, new members might be enrolled. The Central Committee stressed that during Party Weeks only industrial workers, peasants, and Red Army and Navy men should be admitted into the Party. As a result of Party Weeks, over 200,000 joined the Party in 38 gubernias of the European part of the R.S.F.S.R., more than a half of them being industrial workers. Over 25 per cent of the armed forces' strength joined the Party at the fronts.

[24] See LCW, Vol. 30, pp. 253–75.

[25] The *Communist International* a journal, organ of the Executive Committee of the Communist International. It was published in Russian, German, French, English, Spanish and Chinese, the first issue appearing on May 1, 1919.

The journal published theoretical articles and documents of the Comin tern, including a number of articles by Lenin. It elucidated the fundamental questions of Marxist-Leninist theory in connection with problems confronting the international working-class and communist movement and the experience of socialist construction in the Soviet Union. It also waged a struggle against various anti-Leninist tendencies.

Publication of the journal ceased in June 1943 in connection with the resolution adopted by the Presidium of the Comin tern's Executive Committee on May 15, 1943, on the dissolution of the Communist International.

[26] See Karl Marx and Frederick Engels, *Selected Correspondence*, Moscow, 1965, p. 110.

[27] The *Industrial Workers* of the World (I.W.W.) a workers' trade union organization, founded in the U.S.A. in 1905 and in the main organizing unskilled and low-paid workers of various trades. Among its founders were such working-class leaders as Daniel De Leon, Eugene Debs and William Haywood. I.W.W. organizations were also set up in Canada, Australia, Britain, Latin America, and South Africa. In conditions of the mass strike movement in the U.S.A., which developed under the influence of the Russian revolution of 1905–07, the I.W.W. organized a number of successful mass strikes, waged a struggle against the policy of class collaboration conducted by reformist leaders of the American Federation of Labor and Right-wing socialists. During the First World War of 1914–18, the organization led a number of mass anti-war actions by the American working class. Some I.W.W. Leaders, among them William Haywood, welcomed the Great October Socialist Revolution and joined the Communist Party of the U.S.A. At the same time, anarcho-syndicalist features showed up in I.W.W. activities: it did not recognize the proletariat's political struggle, denied the Party's leading role and the necessity of the proletarian dictatorship, and refused to carry on work among the membership of the American Federation of Labor. In 1920 the organization's anarcho-syndicalist leaders took advantage of the imprisonment of many revolutionaries and against the will of the trade union masses, rejected appeal by the Comin tern's Executive Committee that they join the Communist

International. As a result of the leaders' opportunist policy, the I.W.W. degenerated into a sectarian organization, which soon lost all influence on the working-class movement.

[*4] The Gomperses, Hendersons, Jouhaux and Legiens are nothing but Zubatovs, differing from our Zubatov only in their European garb and polish, and the civilised, refined and democratically suave manner of conducting their despicable policy.

Should We Participate In Bourgeois Parliaments?

It is with the utmost contempt and the utmost levity that the German "Left" Communists reply to this question in the negative. Their arguments? In the passage quoted above we read:

> ". . . All reversion to parliamentary forms of struggle, which have become historically and politically obsolete, must be emphatically rejected. . .."

This is said with ridiculous pretentiousness and is patently wrong. "Reversion" to parliamentarianism, forsooth! Perhaps there is already a Soviet republic in Germany? It does not look like it! How, then, can one speak of "reversion"? Is this not an empty phrase?

Parliamentarianism has become "historically obsolete". That is true in the propaganda sense. However, everybody knows that this is still a far cry from overcoming it in practice. Capitalism could have been declared and with full justice to be "historically obsolete" many decades ago, but that does not at all remove the need for a very long and very persistent struggle on the basis of capitalism. Parliamentarianism is "historically obsolete" from the standpoint of *world history*, i.e., the era of bourgeois parliamentarianism is over, and the era of the proletarian dictatorship has begun. That is incontestable. But world history is counted in decades. Ten or twenty years earlier or later makes no difference when measured with the yardstick of world history; from the standpoint of world history, it is a trifle that cannot be considered even approximately. But for that very reason, it is a glaring theoretical error to apply the yardstick of world history to practical politics.

Is parliamentarianism "politically obsolete"? That is quite a different matter. If that were true, the position of the "Lefts" would be a strong one. But it has to be proved by a most searching analysis, and the "Lefts" do not even know how to approach the matter. In the "Theses on Parliamentarianism", published in the *Bulletin of the Provisional Bureau in Amsterdam of the Communist International* No. 1, February 1920, and obviously expressing the Dutch-Left or Left-Dutch strivings, the analysis, as we shall see, is also hopelessly poor.

In the first place, contrary to the opinion of such outstanding political leaders as Rosa Luxemburg and Karl Liebknecht, the German "Lefts", as we know, considered parliamentarianism "politically obsolete" even in January 1919. We know that the "Lefts" were mistaken. This fact alone utterly destroys, at a single stroke, the proposition that parliamentarianism is "politically obsolete". It is for the "Lefts" to prove why their error, indisputable at that time, is no longer an error. They do not and cannot produce even a shred of proof. A political party's attitude towards its own mistakes is one of the most important and surest ways of judging how earnest the party is and how it fulfils in practice its obligations towards its class and the *working people*. Frankly acknowledging a mistake, ascertaining the reasons for it, analyzing the conditions that have led up to it, and thrashing out the means of its rectification that is the hallmark of a serious party; that is how it should perform its duties, and how it should educate and train its *class*, and then the *masses*. By failing to fulfil this duty and give the utmost attention and consideration to the study of their patent error, the "Lefts" in Germany (and in Holland) have proved that they are not a *party of a class*, but a circle, not a *party of the masses*, but a group of intellectualists and of a few workers who are the worst features of intellectualism.

Second, in the same pamphlet of the Frankfurt group of "Lefts", which we have already cited in detail, we read:

> ". . . The millions of workers who still follow the policy of the Centre (the Catholic 'Centre' Party) are counter revolutionary. The rural proletarians provide the legions of counter-revolutionary troops." (Page 3 of the pamphlet.)

Everything goes to show that this statement is far too sweeping and exaggerated. But the basic fact set forth here is incontrovertible, and its acknowledgment by the "Lefts" is particularly clear evidence of their mistake. How can one say that "parliamentarianism is politically obsolete", when "millions" and "legions" of proletarians are not only still in favour of parliamentarianism in general but are downright "counter-revolutionary"!? It is obvious that parliamentarianism in Germany is not yet politically obsolete. It is obvious that the "Lefts" in Germany have mistaken their desire, their politico-ideological attitude, for objective reality. That is a most dangerous mistake for revolutionaries to make. In Russia where, over a particularly long period and in particularly varied forms, the most brutal and savage yoke of tsarism produced revolutionaries of diverse shades, revolutionaries who displayed amazing devotion, enthusiasm, heroism and will power—in Russia we have observed this mistake of the revolutionaries at very close quarters; we have studied it very attentively and have a first-hand knowledge of it; that is why we can also see it especially clearly in others. Parliamentarianism is of course "politically obsolete" to the Communists in Germany but and that is the whole point, we must not regard what is obsolete to us as something obsolete to a *class, to the masses*. Here again we find that the "Lefts" do not know how to reason, do not know how to act as the party of a class, as the party of the masses. You must not sink to the level of the masses, to the level of the backward strata of the class. That is incontestable. You must tell them the bitter truth. You are in duty bound to call their bourgeois-democratic and parliamentary prejudices what they are prejudices. But at the same time, you must *soberly* follow the actual state of the class-consciousness and preparedness of the entire class (not only of its communist vanguard), and of all the working people (not only of their advanced elements).

Even if only a fairly large *minority* of the industrial workers, and not "millions" and "legions", follow the lead of the Catholic clergy and a similar minority of rural workers follow the landowners and kulaks (Grossbauern), it *undoubtedly* signifies that parliamentarianism in Germany has not yet politically outlived itself, that participation in parliamentary elections and in the struggle on the parliamentary rostrum is obligatory on the party of the revolutionary proletariat *specifically* for the purpose of educating the backward strata of its own class, and for the purpose of awakening and enlightening the undeveloped, downtrodden and ignorant rural *masses*. Whilst you lack the strength to do away with bourgeois parliaments and every other type of reactionary institution, you *must* work within them because it is there that you will still find workers who are duped by the priests and stultified by the conditions of rural life otherwise you risk turning into nothing but windbags.

Third, the "Left" Communists have a great deal to say in praise of us Bolsheviks. One sometimes feels like telling them to praise us less and to try to get a better knowledge of the Bolsheviks' tactics. We took part in the elections to the Constituent Assembly, the Russian bourgeois parliament in September–November 1917. Were our tactics correct or not? If not, then this should be clearly stated and proved, for it is necessary in evolving the correct tactics for international communism. If they were correct, then certain conclusions must be drawn. Of course, there can be no question of placing conditions in Russia on a par with conditions in Western Europe. But as regards the particular question of the meaning of the concept that "parliamentarianism has become politically obsolete", due account should be taken of our experience, for unless concrete experience is taken into account such concepts very easily turn into empty phrases. In September–November 1917, did we, the Russian Bolsheviks, not have *more* right than any Western Communists to consider that parliamentarianism was politically obsolete in Russia? Of course, we did for the point is not whether bourgeois parliaments have existed for a long time or a short time, but how far the masses of the working people are *prepared* (ideologically, politically, and practically) to accept the Soviet system and to dissolve the bourgeois-democratic parliament (or allow it to be dissolved). It is an absolutely incontestable and fully established historical fact that, in September–November 1917, the urban working class and the soldiers and peasants of Russia were, because of a number of special conditions, exceptionally well prepared to accept the Soviet system and to disband the most democratic of bourgeois parliaments. Nevertheless, the Bolsheviks did *not* boycott the Constituent Assembly, but took part in the elections both before and *after* the proletariat conquered political power. That these elections yielded exceedingly valuable (and to the proletariat, highly useful) political results has, I make bold to hope, been proved by me in the above-mentioned article, which analyses in detail the returns of the elections to the Constituent Assembly in Russia.

The conclusion which follows from this is absolutely incontrovertible: it has been proved that, far from causing harm to the revolutionary proletariat, participation in a bourgeois-democratic parliament, even a few weeks before the victory of a Soviet republic and even *after* such a victory, actually helps that proletariat to prove to the backward masses why such parliaments deserve to be done away with; it *facilitates* their successful dissolution, and helps to make bourgeois parliamentarianism "politically obsolete". To ignore this experience, while at the same time claiming affiliation to the Communist *International*, which must work out its tactics internationally (not as narrow or exclusively national tactics, but as international tactics), means committing a gross error and actually abandoning internationalism in deed, while recognizing it in word.

Now let us examine the "Dutch-Left" arguments in favour of non-participation in parliaments. The following is the text of Thesis No. 4, the most important of the above-mentioned "Dutch" theses:

> "When the capitalist system of production has broken down, and society is in a state of revolution, parliamentary action gradually loses importance as compared with the action of the masses themselves. When, in these conditions, parliament becomes the centre and organ of the counter-revolution, whilst, on the other hand, the labouring class builds up the instruments of its power in the Soviets, it may even prove necessary to abstain from all and any participation in parliamentary action."

The first sentence is obviously wrong, since action by the masses, a big strike, for instance, is more important than parliamentary activity at *all* times, and not only during a revolution or in a revolutionary situation. This obviously untenable and historically and politically incorrect argument merely shows very clearly that the authors completely ignore both the general European experience (the French experience before the revolutions of 1848 and 1870; the German experience of 1878–90, etc.) and the Russian experience (see above) of the importance of *combining* legal and illegal struggle. This question is of immense importance both in general and in particular, because in *all civilized* and advanced countries the time is rapidly approaching when such a combination will more and more become and has already partly become mandatory on the party of the revolutionary proletariat, inasmuch as civil war between the proletariat and the bourgeoisie is maturing and is imminent, and because of savage persecution of the Communists by republican governments and bourgeois governments generally, which resort to any violation of legality (the example of America is edifying enough), etc. The Dutch, and the Lefts in general, have utterly failed to understand this highly important question.

The second sentence is, in the first place, historically wrong. We Bolsheviks participated in the most counterrevolutionary parliaments, and experience has shown that this participation was not only useful but indispensable to the party of the revolutionary proletariat, after the first bourgeois revolution in Russia (1905), so as to pave the way for the second bourgeois revolution (February 1917), and then for the socialist revolution (October 1917). In the second place, this sentence is amazingly illogical. If a parliament becomes an organ and a "centre" (in reality it never has been and never can be a "centre", but that is by the way) of counter-revolution, while the workers are building up the instruments of their power in the form of the Soviets, then it follows that the workers must prepare ideologically, politically, and technically for the struggle of the Soviets against parliament, for the dispersal of parliament by the Soviets. But it does not at all follow that this dispersal is hindered, or is not facilitated, by the presence of a Soviet opposition *within* the counter-revolutionary parliament. In the course of our victorious struggle against Denikin and Kolchak, we never found that the existence of a Soviet and proletarian opposition in their camp was immaterial to our victories. We know perfectly well that the dispersal of the Constituent Assembly on January 5, 1918 was not hampered but was actually facilitated by the fact that, within the counter-revolutionary Constituent Assembly which was about to be dispersed, there was a consistent Bolshevik, as well as an inconsistent, Left Socialist-Revolutionary Soviet opposition. The authors of the theses are engaged in muddled thinking; they have forgotten the experience of many, if not all, revolutions, which shows the great usefulness, during a revolution, of a *combination* of mass action outside a reactionary parliament with an opposition sympathetic to (or, better still, directly supporting) the revolution within it. The Dutch, and the "Lefts" in general, argue in this respect like doctrinaires of the revolution, who have never taken part in a real revolution, have never given thought to the history of revolutions, or have naïvely mistaken subjective "rejection" of a reactionary institution for its actual destruction by the combined operation of a number of objective factors. The surest way of discrediting and damaging a new political (and not only political) idea is to reduce it to absurdity on the plea of defending it. For any truth, if "overdone" (as Dietzgen Senior put it), if exaggerated, or if carried beyond the limits of its actual applicability, can be reduced to an absurdity, and is even bound to become an absurdity under these conditions. That is just the kind of disservice the Dutch and German Lefts are rendering to the new truth of the Soviet form of government being superior to bourgeois-democratic parliaments. Of course, anyone would be in error who voiced the outmoded viewpoint or in general considered it impermissible, in all and any circumstances, to reject participation in bourgeois parliaments. I cannot attempt here to formulate the conditions under which a boycott is useful, since the object of this pamphlet is far more modest, namely, to study Russian experience in connection with certain topical questions of international communist tactics. Russian experience has provided us with one successful and correct instance (1905), and another that was incorrect (1906), of the use of a boycott by the Bolsheviks. Analyzing the first case, we, see that we succeeded in *preventing* a reactionary government from *convening* a reactionary parliament in a situation in which extra-parliamentary revolutionary mass action (strikes in particular) was developing at great speed, when not a single section of the proletariat and the peasantry could support the reactionary government in any way and when the revolutionary proletariat was gaining influence over the backward masses through the strike struggle and through the agrarian movement. It is quite obvious that *this* experience is not applicable to present-day European conditions. It is likewise quite obvious, and the foregoing arguments bear this out that the advocacy, even if with reservations, by the Dutch and the other "Lefts" of refusal to participate in parliaments is fundamentally wrong and detrimental to the cause of the revolutionary proletariat.

In Western Europe and America, parliament has become most odious to the revolutionary vanguard of the working class. That cannot be denied. It can readily be understood, for it is difficult to imagine anything more infamous, vile or treacherous than the behaviour of the vast majority of socialist and Social-Democratic parliamentary deputies during and after the war. It would, however, be not only unreasonable but actually criminal to yield to this mood when deciding *how* this generally recognized evil should be fought. In many countries of Western Europe, the revolutionary mood, we might say, is at present a "novelty", or a "rarity", which has all too long been vainly and impatiently awaited; perhaps that is why people so easily yield to that mood. Certainly, without a revolutionary mood among the masses, and without conditions facilitating the growth of this mood, revolutionary tactics will never develop into action. In Russia, however, lengthy, painful, and sanguinary experience has taught us the truth that revolutionary tactics cannot be built on a revolutionary mood alone. Tactics must be based on a sober and strictly objective appraisal of all the class forces in a particular state (and of the states that surround it, and of *all* states the world over) as well as of the experience of revolutionary movements. It is very easy to show one's "revolutionary" temper merely by hurling abuse at parliamentary opportunism, or merely by repudiating participation in parliaments it's very ease, however, cannot turn this into a solution of a difficult, a very difficult, problem. It is far more difficult to create a really revolutionary parliamentary group in a European parliament than it was in Russia. That stands to reason. But it is only a particular expression of the general truth that it was easy for Russia, in the specific and historically unique situation of 1917, to start the socialist revolution, but it will be more difficult for Russia than for the European countries to *continue* the revolution and bring it to its consummation. I had occasion to point this out already at the beginning of 1918, and our experience of the past two years has entirely confirmed the correctness of this view. Certain specific conditions, viz., (1) the possibility of linking up the Soviet revolution with the ending, as a consequence of this revolution, of the imperialist war, which had exhausted the workers and peasants to an incredible degree; (2) the possibility of taking temporary advantage of the mortal conflict between the world's two most powerful groups of imperialist robbers, who were unable to unite against their Soviet enemy; (3) the possibility of enduring a comparatively lengthy civil war, partly owing to the enormous size of the country and to the poor means of communication; (4) the existence of such a profound bourgeois-democratic revolutionary movement among the peasantry that the party of the proletariat was able to adopt the revolutionary demands of the peasant party (the Socialist-Revolutionary Party, the majority of whose members were definitely hostile to Bolshevism) and realize them at once, thanks to the conquest of political power by the proletariat all these specific conditions do not at present exist in Western Europe, and a repetition of such or similar conditions will not occur so easily. Incidentally, apart from a number of other causes, that is why it is more difficult for Western Europe to *start* a socialist revolution than it was for us. To attempt to "circumvent" this difficulty by "skipping" the arduous job of utilizing reactionary parliaments for revolutionary purposes is absolutely childish. You want to create a new society, yet you fear the difficulties involved in forming a good parliamentary group made up of convinced, devoted and heroic Communists, in a reactionary parliament! Is that not childish? If Karl Liebknecht in Germany and Z. Höglund in Sweden were able, even without mass support from below, to set examples of the truly revolutionary utilization of reactionary parliaments, why should a rapidly growing revolutionary mass party, in the midst of the post-war disillusionment and embitterment of the masses, be unable to *forge* a communist group in the worst of parliaments? It is because, in Western Europe, the backward masses of the workers and to an even greater degree of the small peasants are much more imbued with bourgeois-democratic and parliamentary prejudices than they were in Russia because of that, it is *only* from within such institutions as bourgeois parliaments that Communists can (and must) wage a long and persistent struggle, undaunted by any difficulties, to expose, dispel and overcome these prejudices.

The German "Lefts" complain of bad "leaders" in their party, give way to despair, and even arrive at a ridiculous "negation" of "leaders". But in conditions in which it is often necessary to hide "leaders" underground, the evolution of good "leaders", reliable, tested, and authoritative, is a very difficult matter; these difficulties *cannot be* successfully overcome without combining legal and illegal work, and *without testing the "leaders", among other ways,* in parliaments. Criticism the most keen, ruthless, and uncompromising criticism should be directed, not against parliamentarianism or parliamentary activities, but against those leaders who are unable and still more against those who are *unwilling* to utilize parliamentary elections and the parliamentary rostrum in a revolutionary and communist manner. Only such criticism combined, of course, with the dismissal of incapable leaders and their replacement by capable ones will constitute useful and fruitful revolutionary work that will simultaneously train the "leaders" to be worthy of the working class and of all working people, and train the masses to be able properly to understand the political situation and the often very complicated and intricate tasks that spring from that situation. [*5]

FOOTNOTES

[*5] I have had too little opportunity to acquaint myself with "Left-wing" communism in Italy. Comrade Bordiga and his faction of Abstentionist Communists *(Comunista astensionista)* are certainly wrong in advocating non-participation in parliament. But on one point, it seems to me, Comrade Bordiga is right as far as can be judged from two issues of his paper, Il Soviet (Nos. 3 and 4, January 18 and February 1, 1920), from four issues of Comrade Serrati's excellent periodical, *Comunismo* (Nos. 1–4, October 1–November 30, 1919), and from separate issues of Italian bourgeois papers which I have seen. Comrade Bordiga and his group are right in attacking Turati and his partisans, who remain in a party which has recognized Soviet power and the dictatorship of the proletariat, and yet continue their former pernicious and opportunist policy as members of parliament. Of course, in tolerating this, Comrade Serrati and the entire Italian Socialist Party [28] are making a mistake which threatens to do as much harm and give rise to the same dangers as it did in Hungary, where the Hungarian Turatis sabotaged both the party and the Soviet government [29] from within. Such a mistaken, inconsistent, or spineless attitude towards the opportunist parliamentarians gives rise to "Left-wing" communism, on the one hand, and to a certain *extent* justifies its existence, on the other. Comrade Serrati is obviously wrong when he accuses Deputy Turati of being "inconsistent" (*Comunismo* No. 3), for it is the Italian Socialist Party itself that is inconsistent in tolerating such opportunist parliamentarians as Turati and Co.

[28] From its foundation in 1892, the *Italian Socialist Party* saw a bitter ideological struggle between the opportunist and the revolutionary trends within it. At the Reggio Emilia Congress of 1912, the most outspoken reformists who supported the war and collaboration with the government and the bourgeoisie (Ivanoe Bonomi, Leonida Bissolati and others) were expelled from the party under pressure from the Left wing. After the outbreak of the First World War and prior to Italy's entry into it, the I.S.P. came out against the war and advanced the slogan: "Against war, for neutrality!" In December 1914, a group of renegades including Benito Mussolini, who advocated the bourgeoisie's imperialist policy and supported the war, were expelled from the party. When Italy entered the war on the Entente's side (May 1915), three distinct trends emerged in the Italian Socialist Party: 1) the Right wing, which aided the bourgeoisie in the conduct of the war; 2) the Centre, which united most of party members and came out under the slogan: "No part in the war, and no sabotage of the war" and 3) the Left wing, which took a firmer anti-war stand, but could not organize a consistent struggle against the war. The Left wing did not realize the necessity of converting the imperialist war into a civil war, and of a decisive break with the reformists.

After the October Socialist Revolution in Russia, the Left wing of the I.S.P. grew stronger, and the 16th Party Congress held on October 5–8, 1919, in Bologna, adopted a resolution on affiliation to the Third International. I.S.P. representatives took part in the work of the Second Congress of the Comin tern. After the Congress Centrist Serrati, head of the delegation, declared against a break with the reformists. At the 17th Party Congress in Leghorn in January 1921, the Centrists, who were in the majority, refused to break with the reformists and to accept all the terms of admission into the Comin tern. On January 21, 1921, the Left-wing delegates walked out of the Congress and founded the Communist Party of Italy.

[29] Soviet rule was established in Hungary on March 21, 1919. The socialist revolution in Hungary was a peaceful one, the Hungarian

bourgeoisie being unable to resist the people. Incapable of overcoming its internal and external difficulties, it decided to hand over power for a while to the Right-wing Social-Democrats so as to prevent the development of the revolution. However, the Hungarian Communist Party's prestige had grown so great, and the demands of rank-and-file Social-Democrats for unity with the Communists had become so insistent that the leaders of the Social-Democratic Party proposed to the arrested Communist leaders the formation of a joint government. The Social-Democratic leaders were obliged to accept the terms advanced by the Communists during the negotiations, i.e., the formation of a Soviet government, disarmament of the bourgeoisie, the creation of a Red Army and people's militia, confiscation of the landed estates, the nationalization of industry, an alliance with Soviet Russia, etc.

An agreement was simultaneously signed on the merging of the two parties to form the Hungarian Socialist Party. While the two parties were being merged, errors were made which later became clear. The merger was carried out mechanically, without isolation of the reformist elements.

At its first meeting, the Revolutionary Governmental Council adopted a resolution on the formation of the Red Army. On March 26, the Soviet Government of Hungary issued decrees on the nationalization of industrial enterprises, transport, and the banks; on April 2, a decree was published on the monopoly of foreign trade. Workers' wages were increased by an average of 25 per cent, and an 8-hour working day was introduced. On April 3, land-reform law was issued, by which all estates exceeding 57 hectares in area were confiscated. The confiscated land, however, was not distributed among the land-starved and landless peasants but was turned over to agricultural producers' cooperatives and state farms organized after the reform. The poor peasants, who had hoped to get land, were disappointed. This prevented the establishment of a firm alliance between the proletariat and the peasantry and weakened Soviet power in Hungary.

The Entente imperialists instituted an economic blockade of the Soviet Republic. Armed intervention against the Hungarian Soviet Republic was organized, the advance of interventionist troops stirring up the Hungarian counter revolutionaries. The treachery of the Right-wing Social-Democrats, who entered into an alliance with international imperialism, was one of the causes of the Hungarian Soviet Republic's downfall.

The unfavourable international situation in the summer of 1919, when Soviet Russia was encircled by enemies and therefore could not help the Hungarian Soviet Republic, also played a definite role. On August 1, 1919, as a result of joint actions by the foreign imperialist interventionists and the domestic counterrevolutionaries, Soviet power in Hungary was overthrown.

No Compromises?

In the quotation from the Frankfurt pamphlet, we have seen how emphatically the "Lefts" have advanced this slogan. It is sad to see people who no doubt consider themselves Marxists, and want to be Marxists, forget the fundamental truths of Marxism. This is what Engels who, like Marx, was one of those rarest of authors whose every sentence in every one of their fundamental works contains a remarkably profound content wrote in 1874, against the manifesto of the thirty-three Blanquist Communards:

> "'We are Communists' (the Blanquist Communards wrote in their manifesto], 'because we want to attain our goal without stopping at intermediate stations, without any compromises, which only postpone the day of victory and prolong the period of slavery.'
>
> "The German Communists are Communists because, through all the intermediate stations and all compromises created, not by them but by the course of historical development, they clearly perceive and constantly pursue the final aim the abolition of classes and the creation of a society in which there will no longer be private ownership of land or of the means of production. The thirty-three Blanquists are Communists just because they imagine that, merely because they want to skip the intermediate stations and compromises, the matter is settled, and if 'it's begins' in the next few days which they take for granted and they

> take overpower, 'communism will be introduced' the day after tomorrow. If that is not immediately possible, they are not Communists.
>
> "What childish innocence it is to present one's own impatience as a theoretically convincing argument!" (Frederick Engels, "Programme of the Blanquist Communards",[30] from the German Social-Democratic newspaper Volksstaat, 1874, No. 73, given in the Russian translation of Articles, 1871–1875, Petrograd, 1919, pp. 52–53).

In the same article, Engels expresses his profound esteem for Vaillant, and speaks of the "unquestionable merit" of the latter (who, like Guesde, was one of the most prominent leaders of international socialism until their betrayal of socialism in August 1914). But Engels does not fail to give a detailed analysis of an obvious error. Of course, to very young and inexperienced revolutionaries, as well as to petty-bourgeois revolutionaries of even very respectable age and great experience, it seems extremely "dangerous", incomprehensible, and wrong to "permit compromises". Many sophists (being unusually or excessively "experienced" politicians) reason exactly in the same way as the British leaders of opportunism mentioned by Comrade Lansbury: "If the Bolsheviks are permitted a certain compromise, why should we not be permitted any kind of compromise?" However, proletarians schooled in numerous strikes (to take only this manifestation of the class struggle) usually assimilate in admirable fashion the very profound truth (philosophical, historical, political, and psychological) expounded by Engels. Every proletarian has been through strikes and has experienced "compromises" with the hated oppressors and exploiters when the workers have had to return to work either without having achieved anything or else agreeing to only a partial satisfaction of their demands. Every proletarian as a result of the conditions of the mass struggle and the acute intensification of class antagonisms he lives among sees the difference between a compromise enforced by objective conditions (such as lack of strike funds, no outside support, starvation and exhaustion), a compromise which in no way minimizes the revolutionary devotion and readiness to carry on the struggle on the part of the workers who have agreed to such a compromise and, on the other hand, a compromise by traitors who try to ascribe to objective causes their self-interest (strike-breakers also enter into "compromises"!), their cowardice, desire to toady to the capitalists, and readiness to yield to intimidation, sometimes to persuasion, sometimes to sops, and sometimes to flattery from the capitalists. (The history of the British labour movement provides a very large number of instances of such treacherous compromises by British trade union leaders, but, in one form or another, almost all workers in all countries have witnessed the same sort of thing.)

Naturally, there are individual cases of exceptional difficulty and complexity, when the greatest efforts are necessary for a proper assessment of the actual character of this or that "compromise", just as there are cases of homicide when it is by no means easy to establish whether the homicide was fully justified and even necessary (as, for example, legitimate self-defense), or due to unpardonable negligence, or even to a cunningly executed perfidious plan. Of course, in politics, where it is sometimes a matter of extremely complex relations national and international between classes and parties, very many cases will arise that will be much more difficult than the question of a legitimate "compromise" in a strike or a treacherous "compromise" by a strike-breaker, treacherous leader, etc. It would be absurd to formulate a recipe or general rule ("No compromises!") to suit all cases. One must use one's own brains and be able to find one's bearings in each particular instance. It is, in fact, one of the functions of a party organization and of party leaders worthy of the name, to acquire, through the prolonged, persistent, variegated and comprehensive efforts of all thinking representatives of a given class, [*6] the knowledge, experience and in addition to knowledge and experience the political flair necessary for the speedy and correct solution of complex political problems. [30]

Naïve and quite inexperienced people imagine that the permissibility of compromise in *general* is sufficient to obliterate any distinction between opportunism, against which we are waging, and must wage, an unremitting struggle, and revolutionary Marxism, or communism. But if such people do not yet know that in nature and in society all distinctions are fluid and up to a certain point conventional, nothing can help them but lengthy training, education, enlightenment, and political and everyday experience. In the practical questions that arise in the politics of any particular or specific historical moment, it is important to single out those which display the principal type of intolerable and treacherous compromises, such as embody an opportunism that is fatal to the revolutionary class, and to exert all efforts to explain them and combat them. During the 1914–18 imperialist war between two groups of equally predatory countries, social-chauvinism was the principal and fundamental type of opportunism, i.e., support of "defence of country", which in such a war was really equivalent to defence of the predatory interests of one's "own" bourgeoisie. After the war, defence of the robber League of Nations, [31] defence of direct or indirect alliances with the bourgeoisie of one's own country against the revolutionary proletariat and the "Soviet" movement, and defence of bourgeois democracy and bourgeois parliamentarianism against "Soviet power" became the principal manifestations of those intolerable and treacherous compromises, whose sum total constituted an opportunism fatal to the revolutionary proletariat and its cause.

> ". . . All compromise with other parties . . . any policy of maneuvering and compromise must be emphatically rejected,"

the German Lefts write in the Frankfurt pamphlet.

It is surprising that, with such views, these Lefts do not emphatically condemn Bolshevism! After all, the German Lefts cannot but know that the entire history of Bolshevism, both before and after the October Revolution, is *full* of instances of changes of tack, conciliatory tactics, and compromises with other parties, including bourgeois parties!

To carry on a war for the overthrow of the international bourgeoisie, a war which is a hundred times more difficult, protracted and complex than the most stubborn of ordinary wars between states, and to renounce in advance any change of tack, or any utilization of a conflict of interests (even if temporary) among one's enemies, or any conciliation or compromise with possible allies (even if they are temporary, unstable, vacillating or conditional allies) is that not ridiculous in the extreme? Is it not like making a difficult ascent of an unexplored and hitherto inaccessible mountain and refusing in advance ever to move in zigzags, ever to retrace one's steps, or ever to abandon a course once selected, and to try others? And yet people so immature and inexperienced (if youth were the explanation, it would not be so bad; young people are preordained to talk such nonsense for a certain period) have met with support whether direct or indirect, open, or covert, whole, or partial, it does not matter from some members of the Communist Party of Holland.

After the first socialist revolution of the proletariat, and the overthrow of the bourgeoisie in some country, the proletariat of that country remains *for a long time weaker* than the bourgeoisie, simply because of the latter's extensive international links, and also because of the spontaneous and continuous restoration and regeneration of capitalism and the bourgeoisie by the small commodity producers of the country which has overthrown the bourgeoisie. The more powerful enemy can be vanquished only by exerting the utmost effort, and by the most thorough, careful, attentive, skillful and obligatory use of any, even the smallest, rift between the enemies, any conflict of interests among the bourgeoisie of the various countries and among the various groups or types of bourgeoisie within the various countries, and also by taking advantage of any, even the smallest, opportunity of winning a mass ally, even though this ally is temporary, vacillating, unstable, unreliable and conditional. Those who do not understand this reveal a failure to understand even the smallest grain of Marxism, of modern scientific socialism *in general.* Those who have not proved *in practice*, over a fairly considerable period of time and in fairly varied political situations, their ability to apply this truth in practice have not yet learned to help the revolutionary class in its struggle to emancipate all toiling humanity from the exploiters. And this applies equally to the period *before* and *after* the proletariat has won political power.

Our theory is not a dogma, but a *guide to action*, said Marx and Engels. [32] The greatest blunder, the greatest crime, committed by such "out-and-out" Marxists as Karl Kautsky, Otto Bauer, etc., is that they have not understood this and have been unable to apply it at crucial moments of the proletarian revolution. "Political activity is not like the pavement of Nevsky Prospekt" (the well-kept, broad, and level pavement of the perfectly straight principal thoroughfare of St. Petersburg), N. G. Chernyshevsky, the great Russian socialist of the pre-Marxist period, used to say. Since Chernyshevsky's time, disregard or forgetfulness of this truth has cost Russian revolutionaries countless sacrifices. We must strive at all costs to *prevent* the Left Communists and West-European and American revolutionaries that are devoted to the working class from paying as *dearly* as the backward Russians did to learn this truth.

Prior to the downfall of tsarism, the Russian revolutionary Social-Democrats made repeated use of the services of the bourgeois liberals, i.e., they concluded numerous practical compromises with the latter. In 1901–02, even prior to the appearance of Bolshevism, the old editorial board of *Iskra* (consisting of Plekhanov, Axelrod, Zasulich, Martov, Potresov and myself) concluded (not for long, it is true) a formal political alliance with Struve, the political leader of bourgeois liberalism, while at the same time being able to wage an unremitting and most merciless ideological and political struggle against bourgeois liberalism and against the slightest manifestation of its influence in the working-class movement. The Bolsheviks have always adhered to this policy. Since 1905 they have systematically advocated an alliance between the working class and the peasantry, against the liberal bourgeoisie and tsarism, never, however, refusing to support the bourgeoisie against tsarism (for instance, during second rounds of elections, or during second ballots) and never ceasing their relentless ideological and political struggle against the Socialist-Revolutionaries, the bourgeois-revolutionary peasant party, exposing them as petty-bourgeois democrats who have falsely described themselves as socialists. During the Duma elections of 1907, the Bolsheviks entered briefly into a formal political bloc with the Socialist-Revolutionaries. Between 1903 and 1912, there were periods of several years in which we were formally united with the Mensheviks in a single Social-Democratic Party, but we *never stopped* our ideological and political struggle against them as opportunists and vehicles of bourgeois influence on the proletariat. During the war, we concluded certain compromises with the Kautskyites, with the Left Mensheviks (Martov), and with a section of the Socialist-Revolutionaries (Chernov and Natanson); we were together with them at Zimmerwald and Kienthal, [33] and issued joint manifestos. However, we never ceased and never relaxed our ideological and political struggle against the Kautskyites, Martov and Chernov (when Natanson died in 1919, a "Revolutionary-Communist" Narodnik, [34] he was very close to and almost in agreement with us). At the very moment of the October Revolution, we entered into an informal but very important (and very successful) political bloc with the petty-bourgeois peasantry by adopting the Socialist-Revolutionary agrarian programme in its *entirety*, without a single alteration i.e., we effected an undeniable compromise in order to prove to the peasants that we wanted, not to "steam-roller" them but to reach agreement with them. At the same time, we proposed (and soon after effected) a formal political bloc, including participation in the government, with the Left *Socialist-Revolutionaries*, who dissolved this bloc after the conclusion of the Treaty of Brest-Litovsk and then, in July 1918, went to the length of armed rebellion, and subsequently of an armed struggle, against us.

It is therefore understandable why the attacks made by the German Lefts against the Central Committee of the Communist Party of

Germany for entertaining the idea of a bloc with the Independents (the Independent Social-Democratic Party of Germany the Kautskyites) are absolutely insane, in our opinion, and clear proof that the "Lefts" are in the *wrong*. In Russia, too, there were Right Mensheviks (participants in the Kerensky government), who corresponded to the German Scheidemanns, and Left Mensheviks (Martov), corresponding to the German Kautskyites and standing in opposition to the Right Mensheviks. A gradual shift of the worker masses from the Mensheviks over to the Bolsheviks was to be clearly seen in 1917. At the First All-Russia Congress of Soviets, held in June 1917, we had only 13 per cent of the votes; the Socialist-Revolutionaries and the Mensheviks had a majority. At the Second Congress of Soviets (October 25, 1917, old style) we had 51 per cent of the votes. Why is it that in Germany the *same and absolutely identical* shift of the workers from Right to Left did not immediately strengthen the Communists, but first strengthened the midway Independent Party, although the latter never had independent political ideas or an independent policy, but merely wavered between the Scheidemanns and the Communists?

One of the evident reasons was the *erroneous* tactics of the German Communists, who must fearlessly and honestly admit this error and learn to rectify it. The error consisted in their denial of the need to take part in the reactionary bourgeois parliaments and in the reactionary trade unions; the error consisted in numerous manifestations of that "Left-wing" infantile disorder which has now come to the surface and will consequently be cured the more thoroughly, the more rapidly and with greater advantage to the organism.

The German Independent Social-Democratic Party is obviously not a homogeneous body. Alongside the old opportunist leaders (Kautsky, Hilferding and apparently, to a considerable extent, Crispien, Ledebour and others), these have revealed their inability to understand the significance of Soviet power and the dictatorship of the proletariat, and their inability to lead the proletariat's revolutionary struggle, there has emerged in this party a Left and proletarian wing, which is growing most rapidly. Hundreds of thousands of members of this party (which has, I think, a membership of some three-quarters of a million) are proletarians who are abandoning Scheidemann and are rapidly going over to communism. This proletarian wing has already proposed at the Leipzig Congress of the Independents (1919) immediate and unconditional affiliation to the Third International. To fear a "compromise" with this wing of the party is positively ridiculous. On the contrary, it is the *duty* of Communists to *seek and find* a suitable form of compromise with them, a compromise which, on the one hand, will facilitate and accelerate the necessary complete fusion with this wing and, on the other, will in no way hamper the Communists in their ideological and political struggle against the opportunist Right wing of the Independents. It will probably be no easy matter to devise a suitable form of compromise but only a charlatan could promise the German workers and the German Communists an "easy" road to victory.

Capitalism would not be capitalism if the proletariat *pur sang* were not surrounded by a large number of exceedingly motley types intermediate between the proletarian and the semi-proletarian (who earns his livelihood in part by the sale of his labour-power), between the semi-proletarian and the small peasant (and petty artisan, handicraft worker and small master in general), between the small peasant and the middle peasant, and so on, and if the proletariat itself were not divided into more developed and less developed strata, if it were not divided according to territorial origin, trade, sometimes according to religion, and so on. From all this follows the necessity, the absolute necessity, for the Communist Party, the vanguard of the proletariat, its class-conscious section, to resort to changes of tack, to conciliation and compromises with the various groups of proletarians, with the various parties of the workers and small masters. It is entirely a matter of *knowing how to* apply these tactics in order to *raise* not lower, the *general* level of proletarian class-consciousness, revolutionary spirit, and ability to fight and win. Incidentally, it should be noted that the Bolsheviks' victory over the Mensheviks called for the application of tactics of changes of tack, conciliation, and compromises, not only before but *also after* the October Revolution of 1917, but the changes of tack and compromises were, of course, such as assisted, boosted, and consolidated the Bolsheviks at the expense of the Mensheviks. The petty-bourgeois democrats (including the Mensheviks) inevitably vacillate between the bourgeoisie and the proletariat, between bourgeois democracy and the Soviet system, between reformism and revolutionism, between love for the workers and fear of the proletarian dictatorship, etc. The Communists' proper tactics should consist in *utilising* these vacillations, not ignoring them; utilising them calls for concessions to elements that are turning towards the proletariat whenever and in the measure that they turn towards the proletariat in addition to fighting those who turn towards the bourgeoisie. As a result of the application of the correct tactics, Menshevism began to disintegrate, and has been disintegrating more and more in our country; the stubbornly opportunist leaders are being isolated, and the best of the workers and the best elements among the petty-bourgeois democrats are being brought into our camp. This is a lengthy process, and the hasty "decision" "No compromises, no manoeuvres", can only prejudice the strengthening of the revolutionary proletariat's influence and the enlargement of its forces.

Lastly, one of the undoubted errors of the German "Lefts" lies in their downright refusal to recognize the Treaty of Versailles. The more "weightily" and "pompously", the more "emphatically" and peremptorily this viewpoint is formulated (by K. Horner, for instance), the less sense it seems to make. It is not enough, under the present conditions of the international proletarian revolution, to repudiate the preposterous absurdities of "National Bolshevism" (Laufenberg and others), which has gone to the length of advocating a bloc with the German bourgeoisie for a war against the Entente. One must realize that it is utterly false tactics to refuse to admit that a Soviet Germany (if a German Soviet republic were soon to arise) would have to recognize the Treaty of Versailles for a time, and to submit to it. From this it does not follow that the Independents at a time when the

Scheidemanns were in the government, when the Soviet government in Hungary had not yet been overthrown, and when it was still possible that a Soviet revolution in Vienna would support Soviet Hungary were right, *under the circumstances*, in putting forward the demand that the Treaty of Versailles should be signed. At that time the Independents tacked and manoeuvred very clumsily, for they more or less accepted responsibility for the Scheidemann traitors, and more or less backslid from advocacy of a ruthless (and most calmly conducted) class war against the Scheidemanns, to advocacy of a "classless" or "above-class" standpoint.

In the present situation, however, the German Communists should obviously not deprive themselves of freedom of action by giving a positive and categorical promise to repudiate the Treaty of Versailles in the event of communism's victory. That would be absurd. They should say: the Scheidemanns and the Kautskyites have committed a number of acts of treachery hindering (and in part quite ruining) the chances of an alliance with Soviet Russia and Soviet Hungary. We Communists will do all we can to *facilitate and pave* the *way* for such an alliance. However, we are in no way obligated to repudiate the Treaty of Versailles, come what may, or to do so at once. The possibility of its successful repudiation will depend, not only on the German, but also on the international successes of the Soviet movement. The Scheidemanns and the Kautskyites have hampered this movement; we are helping it. That is the gist of the matter; therein lies the fundamental difference. And if our class enemies, the exploiters and their Scheidemann and Kautskyite lackeys, have missed many an opportunity of strengthening both the German and the international Soviet movement, of strengthening both the German and the international Soviet revolution, the blame lies with them. The Soviet revolution in Germany will strengthen the international Soviet movement, which is the strongest bulwark (and the only reliable, invincible, and world-wide bulwark) against the Treaty of Versailles and against international imperialism in general. To give absolute, categorical, and immediate precedence to liberation from the Treaty of Versailles and to give it *precedence over the question of liberating other* countries oppressed by imperialism, from the yoke of imperialism, is philistine nationalism (worthy of the Kautskys, the Hilferdings, the Otto Bauers and Co.), not revolutionary internationalism. The overthrow of the bourgeoisie in any of the large European countries, including Germany, would be such a gain for the international revolution that, for its sake, one can, and if necessary, should, tolerate a *more prolonged existence of the Treaty of Versailles.* If Russia, standing alone, could endure the Treaty of Brest-Litovsk for several months, to the advantage of the revolution, there is nothing impossible in a Soviet Germany, allied with Soviet Russia, enduring the existence of the Treaty of Versailles for a longer period, to the advantage of the revolution.

The imperialists of France, Britain, etc., are trying to provoke and ensnare the German Communists: "Say that you will not sign the Treaty of Versailles!" they urge. Like babes, the Left Communists fall into the trap laid for them, instead of skillfully manoeuvring against the crafty and, at *present*, stronger enemy, and instead of telling him, "We shall sign the Treaty of Versailles now." It is folly, not revolutionism, to deprive ourselves in advance of any freedom of action, openly to inform an enemy who is at present better armed than we are whether we shall fight him, and when. To accept battle at a time when it is obviously advantageous to the enemy, but not to us, is criminal; political leaders of the revolutionary class are absolutely useless if they are incapable of "changing tack or offering conciliation and compromise" in order to take evasive action in a patently disadvantageous battle.

FOOTNOTES

[30] See Marx/Engels, *Werke, Dietz Verlag,* Berlin, 1962, Bd. 18, S. 533.

[31] *The League of Nations* was an international body which existed between the First and the Second World Wars. It was founded in 1919 at the Paris Peace Conference of the victor powers of the First World War. The Covenant of the League of Nations formed part of the Treaty

of Versailles of 1919 and was signed by 44 nations. The Covenant was designed to produce the impression that this organization's aim was to combat aggression, reduce armaments and consolidate peace and security. In practice, however, its leaders shielded the aggressors, fostered the arms race and preparations for the Second World War.

Between 1920 and 1934, the League's activities were hostile towards the Soviet Union. It was one of the centres for the organizing of armed intervention against the Soviet state in 1920–21.

On September 15, 1934, on French initiative, 34 member states invited the Soviet Union to join the League of Nations, which the U.S.S.R. did, with the aim of strengthening peace. However, the Soviet Union's attempts to form a peace front met with resistance from reactionary circles in the Western powers. With the outbreak of the Second World War the League's activities came to an end, the formal dissolution taking place in April 1946, according to a decision by the specially summoned Assembly.

[32] Lenin is referring to a passage from Frederick Engels's letter to F. A. Sorge of November 29, 1886, in which, criticizing German Social-Democrat political exiles living in America, Engels wrote that for them the theory was "a credo, not a guide to action" (see Karl Marx and Frederick Engels, *Selected Correspondence, Moscow,* 1965, p. 395).

[33] The reference is to the international socialist conferences in Zimmerwald and Kienthal (Switzerland).

The *Zimmerwald Conference,* the first international socialist conference, was held on September 5–8, 1915. The *Kienthal* Conference, the second international socialist conference, was held in the small town of Kienthal on April 24–30, 1916.

The Zimmerwald and Kienthal conferences contributed to the ideological unity, on the basis of Marxism-Leninism, of the Left-wing elements in West-European Social-Democracy, who later played an active part in the formation of Communist parties in their countries and the establishment of the Third, Communist International.

[34] "*Revolutionary Communists*", a Narodnik group which broke away from the Left Socialist-Revolutionaries after the latter's mutiny in July 1918. In September 1918, they formed the "Party of Revolutionary Communism", which favoured co-operation with the R.C.P.(B.), and pledged support for Soviet power. Their programme which remained on the platform of Narodnik utopianism was muddled and eclectic. While recognizing that Soviet rule created preconditions for the establishment of a socialist system, the "revolutionary communists" denied the necessity of the proletarian dictatorship during the transitional period from capitalism to socialism. Throughout the lifetime of the "Party of Revolutionary Communism", certain of its groups broke away from it, some of them joining the R.C.P.(B.) (A. Kolegayev, A. Bitsenko, M. Dobrokhotov and others), and others, the Left Socialist-Revolutionaries. Two representatives of the "Party of Revolutionary Communism" were allowed to attend the Second Congress of the Comin tern, in a deliberative capacity, but with no votes. In September 1920, following the Congress decision that there must be a single Communist Party in each country, the "Party of Revolutionary Communism" decided to join the R.C.P.(B.). In October of the same year, the R.C.P.(B.) Central Committee permitted Party organizations to enroll members of the former "Party of Revolutionary Communism" in the R.C.P.(B.).

[*6] Within every class, even in the conditions prevailing in the most enlightened countries, even within the most advanced class, and even when the circumstances of the moment have aroused all its spiritual forces to an exceptional degree, there always are and inevitably *will be* as long as classes exist, as long as a classless society has not fully consolidated itself, and has not developed on its own foundations representatives of the class who do not think, and are incapable of thinking, for themselves. Capitalism would not be the Oppressor of the masses that it actually is if things were otherwise.

"Left-Wing" Communism In Great Britain

There is no Communist Party in Great Britain as yet, but there is a fresh, broad, powerful, and rapidly growing communist movement among the workers, which justifies the best hopes. There are several political parties and organizations (the British Socialist Party[35], the Socialist Labour Party, the South Wales Socialist Society, the Workers' Socialist Federation[36]), which desire to form a Communist Party and are already negotiating among themselves to this end. In its issue of February 21, 1920, Vol. VI, No. 48, *The Workers' Dreadnought*, weekly organ of the last of the organizations mentioned, carried an article by the editor, Comrade Sylvia Pankhurst, entitled "Towards a Communist Party". The article outlines the progress of the negotiations between the four organizations mentioned, for the formation of a united Communist Party, on the basis of affiliation to the Third International, the recognition of the Soviet system instead of parliamentarianism, and the recognition of the dictatorship of the proletariat. It appears that one of the greatest obstacles to the immediate formation of a united Communist Party is presented by the disagreement on the questions of participation in Parliament and on whether the new Communist Party should affiliate to the old, trade unionist, opportunist, and social-chauvinist Labour Party, which is mostly made up of trade unions. The Workers' Socialist Federation and the Socialist Labour Party [*7] are opposed to taking part in parliamentary elections and in Parliament, and they are opposed to affiliation to the labour Party; in this they disagree with all or with most of the members of the British Socialist Party, which they regard as the "Right wing of the Communist parties" in Great Britain. (Page 5, Sylvia Pankhurst's article.)

Thus, the main division is the same as in Germany, notwithstanding the enormous difference in the forms in which the disagreements manifest themselves (in Germany the form is far closer to the "Russian" than it is in Great Britain), and in a number of other things. Let us examine the arguments of the "Lefts".

On the question of participation in Parliament, Comrade Sylvia Pankhurst refers to an article in the same issue, by Comrade Gallacher, who writes in the name of the Scottish Workers' Council in Glasgow.

> "The above council," he writes, "is definitely anti-parliamentarian, and has behind it the Left wing of the various political bodies. We represent the revolutionary movement in Scotland, striving continually to build up a revolutionary organization within the industries [in various branches of production], and a Communist Party, based on social committees, throughout the country. For a considerable time, we have been sparring with the official parliamentarians. We have not considered it necessary to declare open warfare on them, and they are afraid to open an attack on us.
>
> "But this state of affairs cannot long continue. We are winning all along the line.
>
> "The rank and file of the I.L.P. in Scotland is becoming more and more disgusted with the thought of Parliament, and the Soviets [the Russian word transliterated into English is used] or Workers' Councils are being supported by almost every branch. This is very serious, of course, for the gentlemen who look to politics for a profession, and they are using any and every means to persuade their members to come back into the parliamentary

fold. Revolutionary comrades must not (all italics are the author's) give any support to this gang. Our fight here is going to be a difficult one. One of the worst features of it will be the treachery of those whose personal ambition is a more impelling force than their regard for the revolution. Any support given to parliamentarism is simply assisting to put power into the hands of our British Scheidemanns and Noskes. Henderson, Clynes and Co. are hopelessly reactionary. The official I.L.P. is more and more coming under the control of middle-class Liberals, who . . . have found their 'spiritual home' in the camp of Messrs. MacDonald, Snowden and Co. The official I.L.P. is bitterly hostile to the Third International, the rank and file is for it. Any support to the parliamentary opportunists is simply playing into the hands of the former. The B.S.P. doesn't count at all here. . . . What is wanted here is a sound revolutionary industrial organization, and a Communist Party working along clear, well-defined, scientific lines. If our comrades can assist us in building these, we will take their help gladly; if they cannot, for God's sake let them keep out altogether, lest they betray the revolution by lending their support to the reactionaries, who are so eagerly clamoring for parliamentary 'honours' (?) (the query mark is the author's) and who are so anxious to prove that they can rule as effectively as the 'boss' class politicians themselves."

In my opinion, this letter to the editor expresses excellently the temper and point of view of the young Communists, or of rank and file workers who are only just beginning to accept communism. This temper is highly gratifying and valuable; we must learn to appreciate and support it for, in its absence, it would be hopeless to expect the victory of the proletarian revolution in Great Britain, or in any other country for that matter. People who can give expression to this temper of the masses and are able to evoke such a temper (which is very often dormant, unconscious, and latent) among the masses, should be appreciated and given every assistance. At the same time, we must tell them openly and frankly that a state of mind is by itself insufficient for leadership of the masses in a great revolutionary struggle, and that the cause of the revolution may well be harmed by certain errors that people who are most devoted to the cause of the revolution are about to commit or are committing. Comrade Gallacher's letter undoubtedly reveals the rudiments of *all* the mistakes that are being made by the German "Left" Communists and were made by the Russian "Left" Bolsheviks in 1908 and 1918.

The writer of the letter is full of a noble and working-class hatred for the bourgeois "class politicians" (a hatred understood and shared, however, not only by proletarians but by all working people, by all Kleinen Leuten to use the German expression). In a representative of the oppressed and exploited masses, this hatred is truly the "beginning of all wisdom", the basis of any socialist and communist movement and of its success. The writer, however, has apparently lost sight of the fact that politics is a science and an art that does not fall from the skies or come gratis, and that, if it wants to overcome the bourgeoisie, the proletariat must train its *own* proletarian "class politicians", of a kind in no way inferior to bourgeois politicians.

The writer of the letter fully realizes that only workers' Soviets, not parliament, can be the instrument enabling the proletariat to achieve its aims; those who have failed to understand this are, of course, out-and-out reactionaries, even if they are most highly educated people, most experienced politicians, most sincere socialists, most erudite Marxists, and most honest citizens and fathers of families. But the writer of the letter does not even ask, it does not occur to him to ask whether it is possible to bring about the Soviets' victory over parliament without getting pro-Soviet politicians *into* parliament, without disintegrating parliamentarianism from *within*, without working within parliament for the success of the Soviets in their forthcoming task of dispersing parliament. Yet the writer of the letter expresses the absolutely correct idea that the Communist Party in Great Britain must act on scientific principles. Science demands, first, that the experience of other countries be taken into account, especially if these other countries, which are also capitalist, are undergoing, or have recently undergone, a very similar experience; second, it demands that account be taken of *all* the forces, groups, parties, classes and masses operating in a given country, and also that policy should not be determined only by the desires and views, by the degree of class-consciousness and the militancy of one group or party alone.

It is true that the Hendersons, the Clyneses, the MacDonalds and the Snowdens are hopelessly reactionary. It is equally true that they want to assume power (though they would prefer a coalition with the bourgeoisie), that they want to "rule" along the old bourgeois lines, and that when they are in power, they will certainly behave like the Scheidemanns and Noskes. All that is true. But it does not at all follow that to support them means treachery to the revolution; what does follow is that, in the interests of the revolution, working-class revolutionaries should give these gentlemen a certain amount of parliamentary support. To explain this idea, I shall take two contemporary British political documents: (1) the speech delivered by Prime Minister Lloyd George on March 18, 1920 (as reported in *The Manchester Guardian* of March 19, 1920), and (2) the arguments of a "Left" Communist, Comrade Sylvia Pankhurst, in the article mentioned above.

In his speech Lloyd George entered into a polemic with Asquith (who had been especially invited to this meeting but declined to attend) and with those Liberals who want, not a coalition with the Conservatives, but closer relations with the Labour Party. (In the above-quoted letter, Comrade Gallacher also points to the fact that Liberals are joining the Independent Labour Party.) Lloyd George argued that a coalition and a close coalition at that between the Liberals and the Conservatives was essential, otherwise there might be a victory for the Labour Party, which Lloyd George prefers to call "Socialist", and which is working for the "*common ownership*" of the means of production. "It is . . . known as communism in France," the leader of the British bourgeoisie said, putting it popularly for his audience, Liberal M.P.s who probably never knew it before. In Germany it was called socialism, and in Russia it is called Bolshevism, he went on to say. To Liberals this is unacceptable on principle, Lloyd George explained, because they stand in principle for private property. "Civilization is in jeopardy," the speaker declared, and consequently Liberals and Conservatives must unite. . . .

> ". . . If you go to the agricultural areas," said Lloyd George, "I agree you have the old party divisions as strong as ever. They are removed from the danger. It does not walk their lanes. But when they see it, they will be as strong as some of these industrial constituencies are now. Four-fifths of this country is industrial and commercial; hardly one-fifth is agricultural. It is one of the things I have constantly in my mind when I think of the dangers of the future here. In France the population is agricultural, and you have a solid body of opinion which does not move very rapidly, and which is not very easily excited by revolutionary movements. That is not the case here. This country is more top-heavy than any country in the world, and if it begins to rock, the crash here, for that reason, will be greater than in any land."

From this the reader will see that Mr. Lloyd George is not only a very intelligent man, but one who has also learned a great deal from the Marxists. We too have something to learn from Lloyd George.

Of definite interest is the following episode, which occurred in the course of the discussion after Lloyd George's speech:

> "Mr. Wallace, M.P.: I should like to ask what the Prime Minister considers the effect might be in the industrial constituencies upon the industrial workers, so many of whom are Liberals at the present time and from whom we get so much support. Would not a possible result be to cause an immediate overwhelming accession of strength

to the Labour Party from men who at present are our cordial supporters?

"The Prime Minister: I take a totally different view. The fact that Liberals are fighting among themselves undoubtedly drives a very considerable number of Liberals in despair to the Labour Party, where you get a considerable body of Liberals, very able men, whose business it is to discredit the Government. The result is undoubtedly to bring a good accession of public sentiment to the Labour Party. It does not go to the Liberals who are outside, it goes to the Labour Party, the by-elections show that."

It may be said, in passing, that this argument shows in particular how muddled even the most intelligent members of the bourgeoisie have become and how they cannot help committing irreparable blunders. That, in fact, is what will bring about the downfall of the bourgeoisie. Our people, however, may commit blunders (provided, of course, that they are not too serious and are rectified in time) and yet in the long run, will prove the victors.

The second political document is the following argument advanced by Comrade Sylvia Pankhurst, a "Left" Communist:

"... Comrade Inkpin (the General Secretary of the British Socialist Party) refers to the Labour Party as 'the main body of the working-class movement'. Another comrade of the British Socialist Party, at the Third International, just held, put the British Socialist Party position more strongly. He said: 'We regard the Labour Party as the organized working class.'

"We do not take this view of the Labour Party. The Labour Party is very large numerically though its membership is to a great extent quiescent and apathetic, consisting of men and women who have joined the trade unions because their workmates are trade unionists, and to share the

> friendly benefits.
>
> "But we recognize that the great size of the Labour Party is also due to the fact that it is the creation of a school of thought beyond which the majority of the British working class has not yet emerged, though great changes are at work in the mind of the people which will presently alter this state of affairs. . . .
>
> "The British Labour Party, like the social-patriotic organizations of other countries, will, in the natural development of society, inevitably come into power. It is for the Communists to build up the forces that will overthrow the social patriots, and in this country, we must not delay or falter in that work.
>
> "We must not dissipate our energy in adding to the strength of the Labour Party; its rise to power is inevitable. We must concentrate on making a communist movement that will vanquish it. The Labour Party will soon be forming a government, the revolutionary opposition must make ready to attack it. . . ."

Thus, the liberal bourgeoisie are abandoning the historical system of "two parties" (of exploiters), which has been hallowed by centuries of experience and has been extremely advantageous to the exploiters and consider it necessary for these two parties to join forces against the Labour Party. A number of Liberals are deserting to the Labour Party like rats from a sinking ship. The Left Communists believe that the transfer of power to the Labour Party is inevitable and admit that it now has the backing of most workers. From this they draw the strange conclusion which Comrade Sylvia Pankhurst formulates as follows:

> "The Communist Party must not compromise. . . . The Communist Party must keep its doctrine pure, and its independence of reformism inviolate, its mission is to lead

> the way, without stopping or turning, by the direct road to the communist revolution."

On the contrary, the fact that most British workers still follow the lead of the British Kerenskys or Scheidemanns and have not yet had experience of a government composed of these people an experience which was necessary in Russia and Germany so as to secure the mass transition of the workers to communism undoubtedly indicates that the British Communists *should* participate in parliamentary action, that they should, from *within* parliament, help the masses of the workers see the results of a Henderson and Snowden government in practice, and that they should help the Hendersons and Snowdens defeat the united forces of Lloyd George and Churchill. To act otherwise would mean hampering the cause of the revolution, since revolution is impossible without a change in the views of the majority of the working class, a change brought about by the political experience of the masses, never by propaganda alone. "To lead the way without compromises, without turning", this slogan is obviously wrong if it comes from a patently impotent minority of the workers who know (or at all events should know) that given a Henderson and Snowden victory over Lloyd George and Churchill, the majority will soon become disappointed in their leaders and will begin to support communism (or at all events will adopt an attitude of neutrality, and, in the main, of sympathetic neutrality, towards the Communists). It is as though 10,000 soldiers were to hurl themselves into battle against an enemy force of 50,000, when it would be proper to "halt", "take evasive action", or even effect a "compromise" so as to gain time until the arrival of the 100,000 reinforcements that are on their way but cannot go into action immediately. That is intellectualist childishness, not the serious tactics of a revolutionary class.

The fundamental law of revolution, which has been confirmed by all revolutions and especially by all three Russian revolutions in the twentieth century, is as follows: for a revolution to take place it is not enough for the exploited and oppressed masses to realize the impossibility of living in the old way, and demand changes; for a revolution to take place it is essential that the exploiters should not be able to live and rule in the old way. It is only when the "*lower classes*" do not want to live in the old way and the "upper classes" *cannot carry on in the old way* that the revolution can triumph. This truth can be expressed in other words: revolution is impossible without a nation-wide crisis (affecting both the exploited and the exploiters). It follows that, for a revolution to take place, it is essential, first, that a majority of the workers (or at least a majority of the class-conscious, thinking, and politically active workers) should fully realize that revolution is necessary, and that they should be prepared to die for it; second, that the ruling classes should be going through a governmental crisis, which draws even the most backward masses into politics (symptomatic of any genuine revolution is a rapid, tenfold and even hundredfold increase in the size of the working and oppressed masses hitherto apathetic, who are capable of waging the political struggle), weakens the government, and makes it possible for the revolutionaries to rapidly overthrow it.

Incidentally, as can also be seen from Lloyd George's speech, both conditions for a successful proletarian revolution are clearly maturing in Great Britain. The errors of the Left Communists are particularly dangerous at present because certain revolutionaries are not displaying a sufficiently thoughtful, sufficiently attentive, sufficiently intelligent, and sufficiently shrewd attitude toward each of these conditions. If we are the party of the revolutionary class, and not merely a revolutionary group, and if we want the *masses* to follow us (and unless we achieve that, we stand the risk of remaining mere windbags), we must, first, help Henderson or Snowden to beat Lloyd George and Churchill (or, rather, compel the former to beat the latter, because the former *are afraid of their victory!)*; second, we must help the majority of the working class to be convinced by their own experience that we are right, i.e., that the Hendersons and Snowdens are absolutely good for nothing, that they are petty-bourgeois and treacherous by nature, and that their bankruptcy is inevitable; third, we must bring nearer the moment when, *on the basis* of the disappointment of most of the workers in the Hendersons, it will be possible, with serious chances of success, to overthrow the government of the Hendersons at once; because if the most astute and solid Lloyd George, that big, not petty, bourgeois, is displaying consternation and is more and more weakening himself (and the bourgeoisie as a whole) by his "friction" with Churchill today and with Asquith tomorrow, how much greater will be the consternation of a Henderson government!

I will put it more concretely. In my opinion, the British Communists should unite their four parties and groups (all very weak, and some of them very, very weak) into a single Communist Party on the basis of the principles of the Third International and of *obligatory* participation in parliament. The Communist Party should propose the following "compromise" election agreement to the Hendersons and Snowdens: let us jointly fight against the alliance between Lloyd George and the Conservatives; let us share parliamentary seats in proportion to the number of workers' votes polled for the Labour Party and for the Communist Party (not in elections, but in a special ballot), and let us retain complete freedom of agitation, propaganda, and political activity. Of course, without this latter condition, we cannot agree to a bloc, for that would be treachery; the British Communists must demand and get complete freedom to expose the Hendersons and the Snowdens in the same way as (*for fifteen years* 1903–17) the Russian Bolsheviks demanded and got it in respect of the Russian Hendersons and Snowdens, i.e., the Mensheviks.

If the Hendersons and the Snowdens accept a bloc on these terms, we shall be the gainers, because the number of parliamentary seats is of no importance to us; we are not out for seats. We shall yield on this point (whilst the Hendersons and especially their new friends or new masters, the Liberals who have joined the Independent Labour Party are most eager to get seats). We shall be the gainers, because we shall carry *our* agitation among the *masses* at a time when Lloyd George *himself* has "incensed" them, and we shall not only be helping the Labour Party to establish its government sooner but shall also be helping the masses sooner to understand the communist propaganda that we shall carry on against the Hendersons, without any reticence or omission.

If the Hendersons and the Snowdens reject a bloc with us on these terms, we shall gain still more, for we shall at once have shown the masses (note that, even in the purely Menshevik and completely opportunist Independent Labour Party, *the rank and file* are in favour of Soviets) that the Hendersons prefer their close relations with the capitalists to the unity of all the workers. We shall immediately gain in the eyes of the masses, who, particularly after the brilliant, highly correct, and highly useful (to communism) explanations given by Lloyd George, will be sympathetic to the idea of uniting all the workers against the Lloyd George-Conservative alliance. We shall gain immediately, because we shall have demonstrated to the masses that the Hendersons and the Snowdens are afraid to beat Lloyd George, afraid to assume power alone, and are striving to secure the secret support of Lloyd George, who is *openly* extending a hand to the Conservatives, against the Labour Party. It should be noted that in Russia, after the revolution of February 27, 1917 (old style), the Bolsheviks' propaganda against the Mensheviks and Socialist-Revolutionaries (i.e., the Russian Hendersons and Snowdens) derived benefit precisely from a circumstance of this kind. We said to the Mensheviks and the Socialist-Revolutionaries: assume full power without the bourgeoisie, because you have a majority in the Soviets (at the First All-Russia Congress of Soviets, in June 1917, the Bolsheviks had only 13 per cent of the votes). But the Russian Hendersons and Snowdens were afraid to assume power without the bourgeoisie, and when the bourgeoisie held up the elections to the Constituent Assembly, knowing full well that the elections would give a majority to the Socialist-Revolutionaries and the Mensheviks [*8] (who formed a close political bloc and in fact represented *only* petty-bourgeois democracy), the Socialist-Revolutionaries and the Mensheviks were unable energetically and consistently to oppose these delays.

If the Hendersons and the Snowdens reject a bloc with the Communists, the latter will immediately gain by winning the sympathy of the masses and discrediting the Hendersons and Snowdens; if, as a result, we do lose a few parliamentary seats, it is a matter of no significance to us. We would put up our candidates in a very few but absolutely safe constituencies, namely, constituencies where our candidatures would not give any seats to the Liberals at the expense of the Labour candidates. We would take part in the election campaign, distribute leaflets agitating for communism, and, in all constituencies where we have no candidates, we would *urge the electors to vote for the Labour candidate and against the bourgeois candidate.* Comrades Sylvia Pankhurst and Gallacher are mistaken in thinking that this is a betrayal of communism, or a renunciation of the struggle against the social traitors. On the contrary, the cause of communist revolution would undoubtedly gain thereby.

At present, British Communists very often find it hard even to approach the masses, and even to get a hearing from them. If I come out as a Communist and call upon them to vote for Henderson and against Lloyd George, they will certainly give me a hearing. And I shall be able to explain in a popular manner, not only why the Soviets are better than a parliament and why the dictatorship of the proletariat is better than the dictatorship of Churchill (disguised with the signboard of bourgeois "democracy"), but also that, with my vote, I want to support Henderson in the same way as the rope supports a hanged man that the impending establishment of a government of the Hendersons will prove that I am right, will bring the masses over to my side, and will hasten the political death of the Hendersons and the Snowdens just as was the case with their kindred spirits in Russia and Germany.

If the objection is raised that these tactics are too "subtle" or too complex for the masses to understand, that these tactics will split and scatter our forces, will prevent us from concentrating them on Soviet revolution, etc., I will reply to the "Left" objectors: don't ascribe your doctrinairism to the masses! The masses in Russia are no doubt no better educated than the masses in Britain; if anything, they are less so. Yet the masses understood the Bolsheviks, and the fact that, in September 1917, on the eve of the Soviet revolution, the Bolsheviks put up their candidates for a bourgeois parliament (the Constituent Assembly) and on *the day after* the Soviet revolution, in November 1917, took part in the elections to this Constituent Assembly, which they got rid of on January 5, 1918 this did not hamper the Bolsheviks, but, on the contrary, helped them.

I cannot deal here with the second point of disagreement among the British Communists, the question of affiliation or non-affiliation to the Labour Party. I have too little material at my disposal on this question, which is highly complex because of the unique character of the British Labour Party, whose very structure is so unlike that of the political parties usual in the European continent. It is beyond doubt, however, first, that in this question, too, those who try to deduce the tactics of the revolutionary proletariat from principles such as: "The Communist Party must keep its doctrine pure, and its independence of reformism inviolate; its mission is to lead the way, without stopping or turning, by the direct road to the communist revolution" will inevitably fall into error. Such principles are merely a repetition of the mistake made by the French Blanquist Communards, who, in 1874, "repudiated" all compromises and all intermediate stages. Second, it is beyond doubt that, in this question too, as always, the task consists in learning to apply the general and basic principles of communism to the *specific relations* between classes and parties, to the specific features in the objective development towards communism, which are different in each country and which we must be able to discover, study, and predict.

This, however, should be discussed, not in connection with British communism alone, but in connection with the general conclusions concerning the development of communism in all capitalist countries. We shall now proceed to deal with this subject.

FOOTNOTES

[35] The British Socialist Party was founded in 1911, in Manchester, as a result of a merger of the Social-Democratic Party and other socialist groups. The B.S.P. conducted agitation in the spirit of Marxism, it was "not opportunist and was really independent of the Liberals". However, its small membership and its poor links with the masses gave the B.S.P. a somewhat sectarian character. During the First World War, a bitter struggle developed within the British Socialist Party between the internationalists (William Gallacher, Albert Inkpin, John Maclean, Theodore Rothstein and others), and the social chauvinists, headed by Hyndman. Within the internationalist trend were inconsistent elements that took a Centrist stand on a number of issues. In February 1916, a group of B.S.P. leaders founded the newspaper The Call, which played an important role in uniting the internationalists. The B.S.P.'s annual conference, held in Salford in April 1916, condemned the social-chauvinist stand of Hyndman and his supporters, who, after the conference, left the party.

The British Socialist Party welcomed the Great October Socialist Revolution, its members playing an important part in the "Hands Off Russia" movement. In 1919, the overwhelming majority of its organizations (98 against 4) declared for affiliation to the Communist International. The British Socialist Party, together with the Communist Unity Group formed the core of the Communist Party of Great Britain. At the First (Unity) Congress, held in 1920. the vast majority of B.S.P. local organizations entered the Communist Party.

[36] *The Socialist Labour* Party was organised in 1903 by a group of the Left-wing Social-Democrats who had broken away from the Social-Democratic Federation. The South Wales Socialist Society was a small group consisting mostly of Welsh coal miners. The Workers' Socialist Federation was a small organization which emerged from the Women's Suffrage League and consisted mostly of women.

The Leftist organizations did not join the Communist Party of Great

Britain when it was formed (its Inaugural Congress was held on July 31–August 1, 1920) since the Party's programme contained a clause on the Party participation in parliamentary elections and on affiliation to the Labour Party. At the Communist Party's Congress in January 1921, the South Wales Socialist Society, and the Workers' Socialist Federation, which had assumed the names of the Communist Workers' Party and the Communist Party respectively, united with the Communist Party of Great Britain under the name of the United Communist Party of Great Britain. The leaders of the Socialist Labour Party refused to join.

[*7] I believe this party is opposed to affiliation to the Labour Party but not all its members are opposed to participation in Parliament.

[*8] The results of the November 1917 elections to the Constituent Assembly in Russia, based on returns embracing over 36,000,000 voters, were as follows: the Bolsheviks obtained 25 per cent of the votes; the various parties of the landowners and the bourgeoisie obtained 13 per cent, and the petty-bourgeois-democratic parties, i.e., the Socialist-Revolutionaries, Mensheviks and a number of similar small groups obtained 62 per cent.

Several Conclusions

The Russian bourgeois revolution of 1905 revealed a highly original turn in world history: in one of the most backward capitalist countries, the strike movement attained a scope and power unprecedented anywhere in the world. In the *first month of 1905 alone*, the number of strikers was ten times the annual average for the previous decade (1895–1904); from January to October 1905, strikes grew all the time and reached enormous proportions. Under the influence of a number of unique historical conditions, backward Russia was the first to show the world, not only the growth, by leaps and bounds, of the independent activity of the oppressed masses in time of revolution (this had occurred in all great revolutions), but also that the significance of the proletariat is infinitely greater than its proportion in the total population; it showed a combination of the economic strike and the political strike, with the latter developing into an armed uprising, and the birth of the Soviets, a new form of mass struggle and mass organization of the classes oppressed by capitalism.

The revolutions of February and October 1917 led to the all-round development of the Soviets on a nation-wide scale and to their victory in the proletarian socialist revolution. In less than two years, the international character of the Soviets, the spread of this form of struggle and organization to the world working-class movement and the historical mission of the Soviets as the grave-digger, heir and successor of bourgeois parliamentarianism and of bourgeois democracy in general, all became clear.

But that is not all. The history of the working-class movement now shows that, in all countries, it is about to go through (and is already going through) a struggle waged by communism emergent, gaining strength and advancing towards victory against, primarily, Menshevism, i.e., opportunism and social chauvinism (the home brand in each particular country), and then as a complement, so to say, Left-wing communism. The former struggle has developed in all countries, apparently without any exception, as a duel between the Second International (already virtually dead) and the Third International. The latter struggle is to be seen in Germany, Great Britain, Italy, America (at any rate, a certain section of the Industrial Workers of the World and of the anarcho-syndicalist trends uphold the errors of Left-wing communism alongside of an almost universal and almost unreserved acceptance of the Soviet system), and in France (the attitude of a section of the former syndicalists towards the political party and parliamentarianism, also alongside of the acceptance of the Soviet system); in other words, the struggle is undoubtedly being waged, not only on an international, but even on a worldwide scale.

But while the working-class movement is everywhere going through what is actually the same kind of preparatory school for victory over the bourgeoisie, it is achieving that development in its *own way* in each country. The big and advanced capitalist countries are travelling this road far *more rapidly* than did Bolshevism, to which history granted fifteen years to prepare itself for victory, as an organized political trend. In the brief space of a year, the Third International has already scored a decisive victory; it has defeated the yellow, social-chauvinist Second International, which only a few months ago was incomparably stronger than the Third International, seemed stable and powerful, and enjoyed every possible support direct and indirect, material (Cabinet posts, passports, the press) and ideological from the world bourgeoisie.

It is now essential that Communists of every country should quite consciously take into account both the fundamental objectives of the struggle against opportunism and "Left" doctrinairism, and the *concrete features* which this struggle assumes and must inevitably assume in each country, in conformity with the specific character of its economics, politics, culture, and national composition (Ireland, etc.), its colonies, religious divisions, and so on and so forth. Dissatisfaction with the Second International is felt everywhere and is spreading and growing, both because of its opportunism and because of its inability or incapacity to create a really centralized and really leading centre capable of directing the international tactics of the revolutionary proletariat in its struggle for a world Soviet republic. It should be clearly realized that such a leading centre can never be built up on stereotyped, mechanically equated, and identical tactical rules of struggle. As long as national and state distinctions exist among peoples and countries and these will continue to exist for a very long time to come, even after the dictatorship of the proletariat has been established on a world-wide scale, the unity of the international tactics of the communist working-class movement in all countries demands, not the elimination of variety or the suppression of national distinctions (which is a pipe dream at present), but an application of the *fundamental* principles of communism (Soviet power and the dictatorship of the proletariat), which will *correctly modify* these principles in certain *particulars*, correctly adapt and apply them to national and national-state distinctions. To seek out, investigate, predict, and grasp that which is nationally specific and nationally distinctive, in the *concrete manner* in which each country should tackle a *single* international task: victory over opportunism and Left doctrinairism within the working-class movement; the overthrow of the bourgeoisie; the establishment of a Soviet republic and a proletarian dictatorship such is the basic task in the historical period that all the advanced countries (and not they alone) are going through. The chief thing though, of course, far from everything the chief thing, has already been achieved: the vanguard of the working class has been won over, has ranged itself on the side of Soviet government and against parliamentarianism, on the side of the dictatorship of the proletariat and against bourgeois democracy. All efforts and all attention should now be concentrated on the next step, which may seem and from a certain viewpoint actually is less fundamental, but, on the other hand, is actually closer to a practical accomplishment of the task. That step is: the search after forms of the *transition* or the *approach* to the proletarian revolution.

The proletarian vanguard has been won over ideologically. That is the main thing. Without this, not even the first step towards victory can be made. But that is still quite a long way from victory. Victory cannot be won with a vanguard alone. To throw only the vanguard into the decisive battle, before the entire class, the broad masses, have taken up a position either of direct support for the vanguard, or at least of sympathetic neutrality towards it and of precluded support for the enemy, would be, not merely foolish but criminal. Propaganda and agitation alone are not enough for an entire class, the broad masses of the working people, those oppressed by capital, to take up such a stand. For that, the masses must have their own political experience. Such is the fundamental law of all great revolutions, which has been confirmed with compelling force and vividness, not only in Russia but in Germany as well. To turn resolutely towards communism, it was necessary, not only for the ignorant and often illiterate masses of Russia, but also for the literate and well-educated masses of Germany, to realize from their own bitter experience the absolute impotence and spinelessness, the absolute helplessness and servility to the bourgeoisie, and the utter vileness of the government of the paladins of the Second International; they had to realize that a dictatorship of the extreme reactionaries (Kornilov[37] in Russia; Kapp[38] and Co. in Germany) is inevitably the only alternative to a dictatorship of the proletariat.

The immediate objective of the class-conscious vanguard of the international working-class movement, i.e., the Communist parties, groups, and trends, is to be able to *lead* the broad masses (who are still, for the most part, apathetic, inert, dormant, and convention-ridden) to their new position, or, rather, to be able to lead, *not only* their own party but also these masses in their advance and transition to the new position. While the first historical objective (that of winning over the class-conscious vanguard of the proletariat to the side of

Soviet power and the dictatorship of the working class) could not have been reached without a complete ideological and political victory over opportunism and social-chauvinism, the second and immediate objective, which consists in being able to lead the masses to a new position ensuring the victory of the vanguard in the revolution, cannot be reached without the liquidation of Left doctrinairism, and without a full elimination of its errors.

As long as it was (and inasmuch as it still is) a question of winning the proletariat's vanguard over to the side of communism, priority went and still goes to propaganda work; even propaganda circles, with all their parochial limitations, are useful under these conditions, and produce good results. But when it is a question of practical action by the masses, of the disposition, if one may so put it, of vast armies, of the alignment of all the class forces in a given society for the final and decisive battle, then propagandist methods alone, the mere repetition of the truths of "pure" communism, are of no avail. In these circumstances, one must not count in thousands, like the propagandist belonging to a small group that has not yet given leadership to the masses; in these circumstances one must count in millions and tens of millions. In these circumstances, we must ask ourselves, not only whether we have convinced the vanguard of the revolutionary class, but also whether the historically effective forces of all classes positively of all the classes in a given society, without exception are arrayed in such a way that the decisive battle is at hand in such a way that: (1) all the class forces hostile to us have become sufficiently entangled, are sufficiently at loggerheads with each other, have sufficiently weakened themselves in a struggle which is beyond their strength; (2) all the vacillating and unstable, intermediate elements, the petty bourgeoisie and the petty-bourgeois democrats, as distinct from the bourgeoisie have sufficiently exposed themselves in the eyes of the people, have sufficiently disgraced themselves through their practical bankruptcy, and (3) among the proletariat, a mass sentiment favouring the most determined, bold and dedicated revolutionary action against the bourgeoisie has emerged and begun to grow vigorously. Then revolution is indeed ripe; then, indeed, if we have correctly gauged all the conditions indicated and summarized above and if we have chosen the right moment, our victory is assured.

The differences between the Churchills and the Lloyd Georges with insignificant national distinctions, these political types exist in all countries on the one hand, and between the Hendersons and the Lloyd Georges on the other, are quite minor and unimportant from the standpoint of pure (i.e., abstract) communism, i.e., communism that has not yet matured to the stage of practical political action by the masses. However, from the standpoint of this practical action by the masses, these differences are most important. To take due account of these differences, and to determine the moment when the inevitable conflicts between these "friends", which weaken and enfeeble all the "*friends*" taken *together*, will have come to a head—that is the concern, the task, of a Communist who wants to be, not merely a class-conscious and convinced propagandist of ideas, but a practical leader of the masses in the revolution. It is necessary to link the strictest devotion to the ideas of communism with the ability to effect all the necessary practical compromises, tacks, conciliatory manoeuvres, zigzags, retreats and so on, in order to speed up the achievement and then loss of political power by the Hendersons (the heroes of the Second International, if we are not to name individual representatives of petty-bourgeois democracy who call themselves socialists); to accelerate their inevitable bankruptcy in practice, which will enlighten the masses in the spirit of our ideas, in the direction of communism; to accelerate the inevitable friction, quarrels, conflicts and complete disintegration among the Hendersons, the Lloyd Georges and the Churchills (the Mensheviks, the Socialist-Revolutionaries, the Constitutional-Democrats, the monarchists; the Scheidemanns, the bourgeoisie and the Kappists, etc.); to select the proper moment when the discord among these "pillars of sacrosanct private property" is at its height, so that, through a decisive offensive, the proletariat will defeat them all and capture political power.

History as a whole, and the history of revolutions in particular, is always richer in content, more varied, more multiform, livelier and more ingenious than is imagined by even the best parties, the most class-conscious vanguards of the most advanced classes. This can readily be understood, because even the finest of vanguards express the class-consciousness, will, passion and imagination of tens of thousands, whereas at moments of great upsurge and the exertion of all human capacities, revolutions are made by the class-consciousness, will, passion and imagination of tens of millions, spurred on by a most acute struggle of classes. Two very important practical conclusions follow from this: first, that in order to accomplish its task the revolutionary class must be able to master all forms or aspects of social activity without exception (completing after the capture of political power sometimes at great risk and with very great danger, what it did not complete before the capture of power); second, that the revolutionary class must be prepared for the most rapid and brusque replacement of one form by another.

One will readily agree that any army which does not train to use all the weapons, all the means and methods of warfare that the enemy possesses, or may possess, is behaving in an unwise or even criminal manner. This applies to politics even more than it does to the art of war. In politics it is even harder to know in advance which methods of struggle will be applicable and to our advantage in certain future conditions. Unless we learn to apply all the methods of struggle, we may suffer grave and sometimes even decisive defeat, if changes beyond our control in the position of the other classes bring to the forefront a form of activity in which we are especially weak. If, however, we learn to use all the methods of struggle, victory will be certain, because we represent the interests of the really foremost and really revolutionary class, even if circumstances do not permit us to make use of weapons that are most dangerous to the enemy, weapons that deal the swiftest mortal blows. Inexperienced revolutionaries often think that legal methods of struggle are opportunist because, in this field, the bourgeoisie has most frequently deceived and duped the workers (particularly in "peaceful" and non-revolutionary times), while illegal methods of struggle are revolutionary. That, however, is wrong. The truth is that those parties and leaders are opportunists and traitors to the working class that are unable or unwilling (do not say, "I can't"; say, "I shan't") to use illegal methods of struggle in conditions such as those which prevailed, for example, during the imperialist war of 1914–18, when the bourgeoisie of the freest democratic countries most brazenly and brutally deceived the workers, and smothered the truth about the predatory character of the war. But revolutionaries who are incapable of combining illegal forms of struggle with every form of legal struggle are poor revolutionaries indeed. It is not difficult to be a revolutionary when revolution has already broken out and is in space, when all people are joining the revolution just because they are carried away, because it is the vogue, and sometimes even from careerist motives. After its victory, the proletariat has to make most strenuous efforts, even the most painful, so as to "liberate" itself from such pseudo-revolutionaries. It is far more difficult and far more precious to be a revolutionary when the conditions for direct, open, really mass and really revolutionary struggle *do not yet exist*, to be able to champion the interests of the revolution (by propaganda, agitation and organization) in non-revolutionary bodies, and quite often in downright reactionary bodies, in a non-revolutionary situation, among the masses who are incapable of immediately appreciating the need for revolutionary methods of action. To be able to seek, find and correctly determine the specific path or the particular turn of events that will *lead* the masses to the real, decisive, and final revolutionary struggle—such is the main objective of communism in Western Europe and in America today.

Britain is an example. We cannot tell no one can tell in advance, how soon a real proletarian revolution will flare up there, and *what immediate cause* will most serve to rouse, kindle, and impel into the struggle the very wide masses, who are still dormant. Hence, it is our duty to carry on all our preparatory work in such a way as to be "well shod on all four feet" (as the late Plekhanov, when he was a Marxist and revolutionary, was fond of saying). It is possible that the breach will be forced, the ice broken, by a parliamentary crisis, or by a crisis arising from colonial and imperialist contradictions, which are hopelessly entangled and are becoming increasingly painful and acute, or perhaps by some third cause, etc. We are not discussing the kind of struggle that will *determine* the fate of the proletarian revolution in Great Britain (no Communist has any doubt on that score for all of us this is a foregone conclusion) what we are discussing is the *immediate cause* that will bring into motion the now dormant proletarian masses and lead them right up to revolution. Let us not forget that in the French bourgeois republic, for example, in a situation which, from both the international and the national viewpoints, was a hundred times less revolutionary than it is today, such an "unexpected" and "petty" cause as one of the many thousands of fraudulent machinations of the reactionary military caste (the Dreyfus case [39]) was enough to bring the people to the brink of civil war!

In Great Britain the Communists should constantly, unremittingly, and unswervingly utilize parliamentary elections and all the vicissitudes of the Irish, colonial, and world-imperialist policy of the British Government, and all other fields, spheres and aspects of public life and work in all of them in a new way, in a communist way, in the spirit of the Third, not the Second, International. I have neither the time nor the space here to describe the "Russian" "Bolshevik" methods of participation in parliamentary elections and in the parliamentary struggle; I can, however, assure foreign Communists that they were quite unlike the usual West-European parliamentary campaigns. From this the conclusion is often drawn: "Well, that was in Russia, in our country parliamentarianism is different." This is a false conclusion. Communists, adherents of the Third International in all countries, exist for the purpose of *changing* all along the line, in all spheres of life, the old socialist, trade unionist, syndicalist, and parliamentary type of work into a *new type* of work, the communist. In Russia, too, there was always an abundance of opportunism, purely bourgeois sharp practices, and capitalist rigging in the elections. In Western Europe and in America, the Communist must learn to create a new, uncustomary, non-opportunist, and non-careerist parliamentarianism; the Communist parties must issue their slogans; true proletarians, with the help of the unorganized and downtrodden poor, should distribute leaflets, canvass workers' houses and cottages of the rural proletarians and peasants in the remote villages (fortunately there are many times fewer remote villages in Europe than in Russia, and in Britain the number is very small); they should go into the public houses, penetrate into unions, societies and chance gatherings of the common people, and speak to the people, not in learned (or very parliamentary) language, they should not at all strive to "get seats" in parliament, but should everywhere try to get people to think, and draw the masses into the struggle, to take the bourgeoisie at its word and utilize the machinery it has set up, the elections it has appointed, and the appeals it has made to the people; they should try to explain to the people what Bolshevism is, in a way that was never possible (under bourgeois rule) outside of election times (exclusive, of course, of times of big strikes, when in Russia a *similar* apparatus for widespread popular agitation worked even more intensively). It is very difficult to do this in Western Europe and extremely difficult in America, but it can and must be done, for the objectives of communism cannot be achieved without effort. We must work to accomplish practical tasks, ever more varied and ever more closely connected with all branches of social life, winning branch after branch, and sphere after sphere *from the bourgeoisie*.

In Great Britain, further, the work of propaganda, agitation, and organization among the armed forces and among the oppressed and underprivileged nationalities in their "own" state (Ireland, the colonies) must also be tackled in a new fashion (one that is not socialist, but communist; not reformist, but revolutionary). That is because, in the era of imperialism in general and especially today after a war that was a sore trial to the peoples and has quickly opened their eyes to the truth (i.e., the fact that tens of millions were killed and maimed for the sole purpose of deciding whether the British or the German robbers should plunder the largest number of countries), all these spheres of social life are heavily charged with inflammable material and are creating numerous causes of conflicts, crises and an intensification of the class struggle. We do not and cannot know which spark of the innumerable sparks that are flying about in all countries as a result of the world economic and political crisis will kindle the conflagration, in the sense of raising up the masses; we must, therefore, with our new and communist principles, set to work to stir up all and sundry, even the oldest, mustiest and seemingly hopeless spheres, for otherwise we shall not be able to cope with our tasks, shall not be comprehensively prepared, shall not be in possession of all the weapons and shall not prepare ourselves either to gain victory over the bourgeoisie (which arranged all aspects of social life and has now disarranged them, in its bourgeois fashion), or to bring about the impending communist reorganization of every sphere of life, following that victory.

Since the proletarian revolution in Russia and its victories on an international scale, expected neither by the bourgeoisie nor the philistines, the entire world has become different, and the bourgeoisie everywhere has become different too. It is terrified of "Bolshevism", exasperated by it almost to the point of frenzy, and for that very reason it is, on the one hand, precipitating the progress of events and, on the other, concentrating on the forcible suppression of Bolshevism, thereby weakening its own position in a number of other fields. In their tactics the Communists in all the advanced countries must take both these circumstances into account.

When the Russian Cadets and Kerensky began furiously to hound the Bolsheviks especially since April 1917, and more particularly in June and July 1917, they overdid things. Millions of copies of bourgeois papers, clamouring in every key against the Bolsheviks, helped the masses to make an appraisal of Bolshevism; apart from the newspapers, all public life was full of discussions about Bolshevism, as a result of the bourgeoisie's "zeal". Today the millionaires of all countries are behaving on an international scale in a way that deserves our heartiest thanks. They are hounding Bolshevism with the same zeal as Kerensky and Co. did; they, too, are overdoing things and *helping* us just as Kerensky did. When the French bourgeoisie makes Bolshevism the central issue in the elections, and accuses the comparatively moderate or vacillating socialists of being Bolsheviks; when the American bourgeoisie, which has completely lost its head, seizes thousands and thousands of people on suspicion of Bolshevism, creates an atmosphere of panic, and broadcasts stories of Bolshevik plots; when, despite all its wisdom and experience, the British bourgeoisie the most "solid" in the world makes incredible blunders, founds richly endowed "anti-Bolshevik societies", creates a special literature on Bolshevism, and recruits an extra number of scientists, agitators and clergymen to combat it, we must salute and thank the capitalists. They are working for us. They are helping us to get the masses interested in the essence and significance of Bolshevism, and they cannot do otherwise, for they have *already* failed to ignore Bolshevism and stifle it.

But at the same time, the bourgeoisie sees practically only one aspect of Bolshevism insurrection, violence, and terror; it therefore strives to prepare itself for resistance and opposition primarily in *this field*. It is possible that, in certain instances, in certain countries, and for certain brief periods, it will succeed in this. We must reckon with such an eventuality, and we have absolutely nothing to fear if it does succeed. Communism is emerging in positively every sphere of public life; its beginnings are to be seen literally on all sides. The "contagion" (to use the favourite metaphor of the bourgeoisie and the bourgeois police, the one mostly to their liking) has very thoroughly penetrated the organism and has completely permeated it. If special efforts are made to block one of the channels, the "contagion" will find another one, sometimes very unexpectedly. Life will assert itself. Let the bourgeoisie rave, work itself into a frenzy, go to extremes, commit follies, take vengeance on the Bolsheviks in advance, and endeavour to kill off (as in India, Hungary, Germany, etc.) more hundreds, thousands, and hundreds of thousands of yesterdays and tomorrow's Bolsheviks. In acting thus, the bourgeoisie is acting as all historically doomed classes have done. Communists should know that, in any case, the future belongs to them; therefore, we can (and must) combine the most intense passion in the great revolutionary struggle, with the coolest and most sober appraisal of the frenzied ravings of the bourgeoisie. The Russian revolution was cruelly defeated in 1905; the Russian Bolsheviks were defeated in July 1917; over 15,000 German Communists were killed as a result of the wily provocation and cunning manoeuvres of Scheidemann and Noske, who were working hand in glove with the bourgeoisie and the monarchist generals; White terror is raging in Finland and Hungary. But in all cases in all countries, communism is becoming steeled and is growing; its roots are so deep that persecution does not weaken or debilitate it but only strengthens it. Only one thing is lacking to enable us to march forward more confidently and firmly to victory, namely, the universal and thorough awareness of all Communists in all countries of the necessity to display the utmost *flexibility* in their tactics. The communist movement, which is developing magnificently, now lacks, especially in the advanced countries, this awareness, and the ability to apply it in practice.

That which happened to such leaders of the Second International, such highly erudite Marxists devoted to socialism as Kautsky, Otto Bauer and others, could (and should) provide a useful lesson. They fully appreciated the need for flexible tactics; they themselves learned Marxist dialectic and taught it to others (and much of what they have done in this field will always remain a valuable contribution to socialist literature); however, *in the application* of this dialectic they committed such an error, or proved to be so undialectical in practice, so incapable of taking into account the rapid change of forms and the rapid acquisition of new content by the old forms, that their fate is not much more enviable than that of Hyndman, Guesde and Plekhanov. The principal reason for their bankruptcy was that they were hypnotized by a definite form of growth of the working-class movement and socialism, forgot all about the one-sidedness of that form, were afraid to see the break-up which objective conditions made inevitable, and continued to repeat simple and, at first glance, incontestable axioms that had been learned by rote, like: "three is more than two". But politics is more like algebra than like arithmetic, and still more like higher than elementary mathematics. In reality, all the old forms of the socialist movement have acquired a new content, and, consequently, a new symbol, the "minus" sign, has appeared in front of all the figures; our wiseacres, however, have stubbornly continued (and still continue) to persuade themselves and others that "minus three" is more than "minus two".

We must see to it that Communists do not make a similar mistake, only in the opposite sense, or rather, we must see to it that a *similar mistake*, only made in the opposite sense by the "Left" Communists, is corrected as soon as possible, and eliminated as rapidly and painlessly as possible. It is not only Right doctrinairism that is erroneous; Left doctrinairism is erroneous too. Of course, the mistake of Left doctrinairism in communism is at present a thousand times less dangerous and less significant than that of Right doctrinairism (i.e., social-chauvinism and Kautskyism); but, after all, that is only due to the fact that Left communism is a very young trend, is only just coming into being. It is only for this reason that, under certain conditions, the disease can be easily eradicated, and we must set to work with the utmost energy to eradicate it.

The old forms burst asunder, for it turned out that their new content, anti-proletarian, and reactionary had attained an inordinate development. From the standpoint of the development of international communism, our work today has such a durable and powerful content (for Soviet power and the dictatorship of the proletariat) that it can and *must* manifest itself in any form, both new and old; it can and must regenerate, conquer and subjugate all forms, not only the new, but also the old, not for the purpose of reconciling itself with the old, but for the purpose of making all and every form new and old, a weapon for the complete and irrevocable victory of communism.

The Communists must exert every effort to direct the working-class movement and social development in general along the straightest and shortest road to the victory of Soviet power and the dictatorship of the proletariat on a world-wide scale. That is an incontestable truth. But it is enough to take one little step farther, a step that might seem to be in the same direction and truth turns into error. We have only to say, as the German and British Left Communists do, that we recognize only one road, only the direct road, and that we will not permit tacking, conciliatory manoeuvres, or compromising and it will be a mistake which may cause, and in part has already caused and is causing, very grave prejudices to communism. Right doctrinairism persisted in recognizing only the old forms, and became utterly bankrupt, for it did not notice the new content. Left doctrinairism persists in the unconditional repudiation of certain old forms, failing to see that the new content is forcing its way through all and sundry forms, that it is our duty as Communists to master all forms, to learn how, with the maximum rapidity, to supplement one form with another, to substitute one for another, and to adapt our tactics to any such change that does not come from our class or from our efforts.

World revolution has been so powerfully stimulated and accelerated by the horrors, vileness and abominations of the world imperialist war and by the hopelessness of the situation created by it, this revolution is developing in scope and depth with such splendid rapidity, with such a wonderful variety of changing forms, with such an instructive practical refutation of all doctrinairism, that there is every reason to hope for a rapid and complete recovery of the international communist movement from the infantile disorder of "Left-wing" communism.

April 27, 1920

FOOTNOTES

[37] This refers to the counter-revolutionary mutiny organized in August 1917 by the bourgeoisie and the landowners, under the Supreme Commander-in-Chief, the tsarist general Kornilov. The conspirators hoped to seize Petrograd, smash the Bolshevik Party, break up the Soviets, establish a military dictatorship in the country, and prepare the restoration of the monarchy.

The mutiny began on August 25 (September 7), Kornilov sending the 3rd Cavalry Corps against Petrograd, where Kornilov counter-revolutionary organizations were ready to act.

The Kornilov mutiny was crushed by the workers and peasants led by the Bolshevik Party. Under pressure from the masses, the Provisional Government was forced to order that Kornilov, and his accomplices be arrested and brought to trial.

[38] The reference is to the military-monarchist coup d'état, the so-called Kapp *putsch* organized by the German reactionary militarists. It was headed by the monarchist landowner Kapp and Generals Ludendorff, Seeckt and Lüttwitz. The conspirators prepared the coup with the connivance of the Social-Democratic government. On March 13, 1920, the mutinous generals moved troops against Berlin and, meeting with no resistance from the government, proclaimed a military dictatorship. The German workers replied with a general strike. Under pressure from the proletariat the Kapp government was overthrown on March 17, and the Social-Democrats again took power.

[39] The *Dreyfus case*, a provocative trial organized in 1894 by the reactionary-monarchist circles of the French militarists. On trial was Dreyfus, a Jewish officer of the French General Staff, falsely accused of espionage and high treason. Dreyfus's conviction, he was condemned to life imprisonment was used by the French reactionaries to rouse anti-Semitism and to attack the republican regime and democratic liberties. When, in 1898, socialists and progressive bourgeois democrats such as Emile Zola, Jean Jaures, and Anatole France launched a campaign for Dreyfus's re-trial, the case became a major political issue and split the country into two camps, the republicans and democrats on the one hand, and a bloc of monarchists, clericals, anti-Semites and nationalists, on the other. Under the pressure of public opinion, Dreyfus was released in 1899, and in 1906 was acquitted by the Court of Cassation and reinstated in the Army.

Appendix

Before publishing houses in our country, which has been plundered by the imperialists of the whole world in revenge for the proletarian revolution, and which is still being plundered and blockaded by them regardless of all promises they made to their workers were able to bring out my pamphlet, additional material arrived from abroad. Without claiming to present in my pamphlet anything more than the cursory notes of a publicist, I shall dwell briefly upon a few points.

I. The Split Among the German Communists

The split among the Communists in Germany is an accomplished fact. The "Lefts", or the "opposition on principle", have formed a separate Communist Workers' Party, as distinct from the Communist Party. A split also seems imminent in Italy I say "seems", as I have only two additional issues (Nos. 7 and 8) of the Left newspaper, Il Soviet, in which the possibility of and necessity for a split is openly discussed, and mention is also made of a congress of the "Abstentionist" group (or the boycottists, i.e., opponents of participation in parliament), which group is still part of the Italian Socialist Party.

There is reason to fear that the split with the "Lefts", the anti-parliamentarians (in part anti-politicals too, who are opposed to any political party and to work in the trade unions), will become an international phenomenon, like the split with the "Centrists" (i.e., Kautskyites, Longuetists, Independents, etc.). Let that be so. At all events, a split is better than confusion, which hampers the ideological, theoretical, and revolutionary growth and maturing of the party, and its harmonious, really organized practical work which actually paves the way for the dictatorship of the proletariat.

Let the "Lefts" put themselves to a practical test on a national and international scale. Let them try to prepare for (and then implement) the dictatorship of the proletariat, without a rigorously centralized party with iron discipline, without the ability to become masters of every sphere, every branch, and every variety of political and cultural work. Practical experience will soon teach them.

Only, every effort should be made to prevent the split with the "Lefts" from impeding or to see that it impedes as little as possible—the necessary amalgamation into a single party, inevitable in the near future, of all participants in the working-class movement who sincerely and conscientiously stand for Soviet government and the dictatorship of the proletariat. It was the exceptional good fortune of the Bolsheviks in Russia to have had fifteen years for a systematic and consummated struggle both against the Mensheviks (i.e., the opportunists and "Centrists") and against the "Lefts", long before the masses began direct action for the dictatorship of the proletariat. In Europe and America, the same work has now to be done by forced marches, so to say. Certain individuals, especially among unsuccessful aspirants to leadership, may (if they lack proletarian discipline and are not honest towards themselves) persist in their mistakes for a long time; however, when the time is ripe, the masses of the workers will themselves unite easily and rapidly and unite all sincere Communists to form a single party capable of establishing the Soviet system and the dictatorship of the proletariat. [*9]

II. The Communists and the Independents in Germany

In this pamphlet I have expressed the opinion that a compromise between the Communists and the Left wing of the Independents is necessary and useful to communism but will not be easy to bring about. Newspapers which I have subsequently received have confirmed this opinion on both points. No. 32 of The Red Flag, organ of the Central Committee, the Communist Party of Germany (*Die Rote Fahne*, Zentralorgan der Kommunistischen Partei Deutschlands, Spartakusbund, of March 26, 1920) published a "statement" by this Central Committee regarding the Kapp-Lüttwitz military putsch and on the "socialist government". This statement is quite correct both in its basic premise and its practical conclusions. The basic premise is that at present there is no "objective basis" for the dictatorship of the proletariat because the "majority of the urban workers" support the Independents. The conclusion is: a promise to be a "loyal opposition" (i.e., renunciation of preparations for a "forcible overthrow") to a "socialist government if it excludes bourgeois-capitalist parties".

In the main, this tactic is undoubtedly correct. Yet, even if minor inaccuracies of formulation should not be dwelt on, it is impossible to pass over in silence the fact that a government consisting of social-traitors should not (in an official statement by the Communist Party) be called "socialist"; that one should not speak of the exclusion of "bourgeois-capitalist parties", when the parties both of the Scheidemanns and of the Kautskys and Crispiens are petty-bourgeois-democratic parties; that things should never be written that are contained in §4 of the statement, which reads:

> ". . . A state of affairs in which political freedom can be enjoyed without restriction, and bourgeois democracy cannot operate as the dictatorship of capital is, from the viewpoint of the development of the proletarian dictatorship, of the utmost importance in further winning the proletarian masses over to the side of communism."

Such a state of affairs is impossible. Petty-bourgeois leaders, the German Hendersons (Scheidemanns) and Snowdens (Crispiens), do not and cannot go beyond the bounds of bourgeois democracy, which, in its turn, cannot but be a dictatorship of capital. To achieve the practical results that the Central Committee of the Communist Party had been quite rightly working for, there was no need to write such things, which are wrong in principle and politically harmful. It would have been sufficient to say (if one wished to observe parliamentary amenities): "As long as the majority of the urban workers follow the Independents, we Communists must do nothing to prevent those workers from getting rid of their last philistine-democratic (i.e., 'bourgeois-capitalist') illusions by going through the experience of having a government of their 'own'." That is sufficient ground for a compromise, which is really necessary and should consist in renouncing, for a certain period, all attempts at the forcible overthrow of a government which enjoys the confidence of a majority of the urban workers. But in everyday mass agitation, in which one is not bound by official parliamentary amenities, one might, of course, add: "Let scoundrels like the Scheidemanns, and philistines like the Kautskys and Crispiens reveal by their deeds how they have been fooled themselves and how they are fooling the workers; their 'clean' government will itself do the 'cleanest' job of all in 'cleansing' the Augean stables of socialism, Social-Democracy and other forms of social treachery."

The real nature of the present leaders of the Independent Social-Democratic Party of Germany (leaders of whom it has been wrongly said that they have already lost all influence, whereas in reality they are even more dangerous to the proletariat that the Hungarian Social-Democrats who styled themselves Communists and promised to "support" the dictatorship of the proletariat) was once again revealed during the German equivalent of the Kornilov revolt, i.e., the Kapp-Lüttwitz putsch. [*10] A small but striking illustration is provided by two brief articles one by Karl Kautsky entitled "Decisive Hours" ("Entscheidende Stunden") in *Freiheit (Freedom)*, organ of the Independents, of March 30, 1920, and the other by Arthur Crispien entitled "On the Political Situation" (in the same newspaper, issue of April 14, 1920). These gentlemen are absolutely incapable of thinking and reasoning like revolutionaries. They are sniveling philistine democrats, who become a thousand times more dangerous to the proletariat when they claim to be supporters of Soviet government and of the dictatorship of the proletariat because, in fact, whenever a difficult and dangerous situation arises, they are sure to commit treachery . . . while "sincerely" believing that they are helping the proletariat! Did not the Hungarian Social-Democrats, after rechristening themselves Communists, also want to "help" the proletariat when, because of their cowardice and spinelessness, they considered the position of Soviet power in Hungary hopeless and went sniveling to the agents of the Entente capitalists and the Entente hangmen?

III. Turati and Co. in Italy

The issues of the Italian newspaper Il Soviet referred to above fully confirm what I have said in the pamphlet about the Italian Socialist Party's error in tolerating such members and even such a group of parliamentarians in their ranks. It is still further confirmed by an outside observer like the Rome correspondent of *The Manchester Guardian*, organ of the British liberal bourgeoisie, whose interview with Turati is published in its issue of March 12, 1920. The correspondent writes:

> ". . . Signor Turati's opinion is that the revolutionary peril is not such as to cause undue anxiety in Italy. The Maximalists are fanning the fire of Soviet theories only to keep the masses awake and excited. These theories are, however, merely legendary notions, unripe programmes, incapable of being put to practical use. They are likely only to maintain the working classes in a state of expectation. The very men who use them as a lure to dazzle proletarian eyes find themselves compelled to fight a daily battle for the extortion of some often-trifling economic advantages so as to delay the moment when the working classes will lose their illusions and faith in their cherished myths. Hence a long string of strikes of all sizes and with all pretexts up to the very latest ones in the mail and railway services strikes which make the already hard conditions of the country still worse. The country is irritated owing to the difficulties connected with its Adriatic problem,

> is weighed down by its foreign debt and by its inflated paper circulation, and yet it is still far from realizing the necessity of adopting that discipline of work which alone can restore order and prosperity."

It is clear as daylight that this British correspondent has blurted out the truth, which is probably being concealed and glossed over both by Turati himself, and his bourgeois defenders, accomplices, and inspirers in Italy. That truth is that the ideas and political activities of Turati, Treves, Modigliani, Dugoni and Co. are really and precisely of the kind that the British correspondent has described. It is downright social treachery. Just look at this advocacy of order and discipline among the workers, who are wage-slaves toiling to enrich the capitalists! And how familiar to us Russians are all these Menshevik speeches! What a valuable admission it is that the masses are in favour of Soviet government! How stupid and vulgarly bourgeois is the failure to understand the revolutionary role of strikes which are spreading spontaneously! Indeed, the correspondent of the British bourgeois-liberal newspaper has rendered Turati and Co. a disservice and has excellently confirmed the correctness of the demand by Comrade Bordiga and his friends on Il Soviet, who are insisting that the Italian Socialist Party, if it really wants to be for the Third International, should drum Turati and Co. out of its ranks and become a Communist Party both in name and in deed.

IV. False Conclusions from Correct Premises

However, Comrade Bordiga and his "Left" friends draw from their correct criticism of Turati and Co. the wrong conclusion that any participation in parliament is harmful in principle. The Italian "Lefts" cannot advance even a shadow of serious argument in support of this view. They simply do not know (or try to forget) the international examples of really revolutionary and communist utilization of bourgeois parliaments, which has been of unquestionable value in preparing for the proletarian revolution. They simply cannot conceive of any "new" ways of that utilization and keep on repeatedly and endlessly vociferating about the "old" non-Bolshevik way.

Herein lies their fundamental error. In *all* fields of activity, and not in the parliamentary sphere alone, communism must *introduce* (and without long and persistent effort it will be *unable* to introduce) something new in principle that will represent a radical break with the traditions of the Second International (while retaining and developing what was good in the latter).

Let us take, say, journalistic work. Newspapers, pamphlets, and leaflets perform the indispensable work of propaganda, agitation, and organization. No mass movement in any country at all civilized can get along without a journalistic apparatus. No outcries against "leaders" or solemn vows to keep the masses uncontaminated by the influence of leaders will relieve us of the necessity of using, for this work, people from a bourgeois-intellectual environment or will rid us of the bourgeois-democratic, "private property" atmosphere and environment in which this work is carried out under capitalism. Even two and a half years after the overthrow of the bourgeoisie, after the conquest of political power by the proletariat, we still have this atmosphere around us, this environment of mass (peasant, artisan) bourgeois-democratic private property relations.

Parliamentarianism is one form of activity; journalism is another. The content of both can and should be communist if those engaged in these two spheres are genuine Communists, really members of a proletarian mass party. Yet, in neither sphere and *in no other sphere of activity* under capitalism and during the period of transition from capitalism to socialism, is it possible to avoid those difficulties which the proletariat must overcome, those special problems which the proletariat must solve so as to use, for its own purposes, the services of people from the ranks of the bourgeoisie, eradicate bourgeois-intellectualist prejudices and influences, and weaken the resistance of (and, ultimately, completely transform) the petty-bourgeois environment.

Did we not, before the war of 1914–18, witness in all countries innumerable cases of extreme "Left" anarchists, syndicalists and others fulminating against parliamentarianism, deriding bourgeois-vulgarized parliamentary socialists, castigating their careerism, and so on and so forth, and yet themselves pursuing the same kind of bourgeois career *through* journalism and *through* work in the syndicates (trade unions)? Is not the example of Jouhaux and Merrheim, to limit oneself to France, typical in this respect?

The childishness of those who "repudiate" participation in parliament consists in their thinking it possible to "solve" the difficult problem of combating bourgeois-democratic influences *within* the working-class movement in such a "simple", "easy", allegedly revolutionary manner, whereas they are actually merely running away from their own shadows, only closing their eyes to difficulties, and trying to shrug them off with mere words. The most shameless careerism, the bourgeois utilization of parliamentary seats, glaringly reformist perversion of parliamentary activity, and vulgar petty-bourgeois conservatism are all unquestionably common and prevalent features engendered everywhere by capitalism, not only outside but also within the working-class movement. But the selfsame capitalism and the bourgeois environment it creates (which disappears very slowly even after the overthrow of the bourgeoisie, since the peasantry constantly regenerates the bourgeoisie) give rise to what is essentially the same bourgeois careerism, national chauvinism, petty-bourgeois vulgarity, etc. merely varying insignificantly in form in positively every sphere of activity and life.

You think, my dear boycottists and anti-parliamentarians, that you are "terribly revolutionary" but in reality, *you are frightened* by the comparatively minor difficulties of the struggle against bourgeois influences within the working-class movement, whereas your victory i.e., the overthrow of the bourgeoisie and the conquest of political power by the proletariat will create these *very same* difficulties on a still larger, an infinitely larger scale. Like children, you are frightened by a minor difficulty which confronts you today, but you do not understand that tomorrow, and the day after, you will still have to learn, and learn thoroughly, to overcome the selfsame difficulties, only on an immeasurably greater scale.

Under Soviet rule, your proletarian party and ours will be invaded by a still larger number of bourgeois intellectuals. They will worm their way into the Soviets, the courts, and the administration, since communism cannot be built otherwise than with the aid of the human material created by capitalism, and the bourgeois intellectuals cannot be expelled and destroyed, but must be won over, remoulded, assimilated and re-educated, just as we must in a protracted struggle waged on the basis of the dictatorship of the proletariat, re-educate the proletarians themselves, who do not abandon their petty-bourgeois prejudices at one stroke, by a miracle, at the behest of the Virgin Mary, at the behest of a slogan, resolution or decree, but only in the course of a long and difficult mass struggle against mass petty-bourgeois influences. Under Soviet rule, these same problems, which the anti-parliamentarians now so proudly, so haughtily, so lightly and so childishly brush aside with a wave of the hand these *selfsame* problems are arising anew *within* the Soviets, within the Soviet administration among the Soviet "pleaders" (in Russia we have abolished, and have rightly abolished, the bourgeois legal bar, but it is reviving again under the cover of the "Soviet pleaders" [40]'). Among Soviet engineers, Soviet schoolteachers and the privileged, i.e., the most highly skilled and best situated, *workers* at Soviet factories, we observe a constant revival of absolutely all the negative traits peculiar to bourgeois parliamentarianism, and we are conquering this evil gradually only by a tireless, prolonged, and persistent struggle based on proletarian organization and discipline.

Of course, under the rule of the bourgeoisie it is very "difficult" to eradicate bourgeois habits from our own, i.e., the workers', party; it is "difficult" to expel from the party the familiar parliamentary leaders who have been hopelessly corrupted by bourgeois prejudices; it is "difficult" to subject to proletarian discipline the absolutely essential (even if very limited) number of people coming from the ranks of the bourgeoisie; it is "difficult" to form, in a bourgeois parliament, a communist group fully worthy of the working class; it is "difficult" to ensure that the communist parliamentarians do not engage in bourgeois parliamentary inanities, but concern themselves with the very urgent work of propaganda, agitation and organization among the masses. All this is "difficult", to be sure; it was difficult in Russia, and it is vastly more difficult in Western Europe and in America, where the bourgeoisie is far stronger, where bourgeois-democratic traditions are stronger, and so on.

Yet all these "difficulties" are mere child's play compared with the *same* sort of problems which, in any event, the proletariat will have most certainly to solve in order to achieve victory, both during the proletarian revolution and after the seizure of power by the proletariat. Compared with these truly gigantic problems of re-educating, under the proletarian dictatorship, millions of peasants and small proprietors, hundreds of thousands of office employees, officials and bourgeois intellectuals, of subordinating them all to the proletarian state and to proletarian leadership, of eradicating their bourgeois habits and traditions compared with these gigantic problems it is childishly easy to create, under the rule of the bourgeoisie, and in a bourgeois parliament, a really communist group of a real proletarian party.

If our "Left" and anti-parliamentarian comrades do not learn to overcome even such a small difficulty now, we may safely assert that either they will prove incapable of achieving the dictatorship of the proletariat, and will be unable to subordinate and remould the bourgeois intellectuals and bourgeois institutions on a wide scale, or they will have to hastily complete their education, and, by that haste, will do a great deal of harm to the cause of the proletariat, will commit more errors than usual, will manifest more than average weakness and inefficiency, and so on and so forth.

Until the bourgeoisie has been overthrown and, after that, until small-scale economy and small commodity production have entirely disappeared, the bourgeois atmosphere, proprietary habits and petty-bourgeois traditions will hamper proletarian work both outside and within the working-class movement, not only in a single field of activity, the parliamentary but, inevitably, in every field of social activity, in all cultural and political spheres without exception. The attempt to brush aside, to fence oneself off from one of the "unpleasant" problems or difficulties in some one sphere of activity is a profound mistake, which will later most certainly have to be paid for. We must learn how to master every sphere of work and activity without exception, to overcome all difficulties and eradicate all bourgeois habits, customs, and traditions everywhere. Any other way of presenting the question is just trifling, mere childishness.

May 12, 1920

V.

In the Russian edition of this book, I somewhat incorrectly described the conduct of the Communist Party of Holland as a whole, in the sphere of international revolutionary policy. I therefore avail myself of the present opportunity to publish a letter from our Dutch comrades on this question and to correct the expression "Dutch Tribunists", which I used in the Russian text, and for which I now substitute the words "certain members of the Communist Party of Holland." [41]

N. Lenin

Letter From Wijnkoop

Moscow, June 30, 1920

Dear Comrade Lenin,

Thanks to your kindness, we members of the Dutch delegation to the Second Congress of the Communist International were able to read your "*Left-Wing*" *Communism—An Infantile* Disorder prior to its publication in the European languages. In several places in the book, you emphasize your disapproval of the part played by some members of the Communist Party of Holland in international politics.

We feel, nevertheless, that we must protest against your laying the responsibility for their actions on the Communist Party. This is highly inaccurate. Moreover, it is unjust, because these members of the Communist Party of Holland take little or no part in the Party's current activities and are endeavouring, directly or indirectly, to give effect, in the Communist Party of Holland, to opposition slogans against which the Party and all its organs have waged, and continue to wage to this day, a most energetic struggle.

Fraternally yours,

D. J. Wijnkoop

(On behalf of the Dutch delegation)

FOOTNOTES

[40] "*Soviet pleaders*", collegiums of advocates established in February 1918, under the Soviets of Workers', Soldiers', Peasants', and Cossacks' Deputies. In October 1920, these collegiums were abolished.

[41] On the basis of this directive from Lenin the words "certain members of the Communist Party of Holland" have been substituted everywhere in this volume, in the text of "*Left-Wing*" Communism, an Infantile Disorder for the expression "Dutch Tribunists".

[*9] With regard to the question of future amalgamation of the "Left" Communists, the anti-parliamentarians, with the Communists in general, I would make the following additional remarks. In the measure in which I have been able to familiarize myself with the newspapers of the "Left" Communists and the Communists in general in Germany, I find that the former have the advantage of being better able than the latter to carry on agitation among the masses. I have repeatedly observed something similar to this in the history

of the Bolshevik Party, though on a smaller scale, in individual local organizations, and not on a national scale. For instance, in 1907–08 the "Left" Bolsheviks, on certain occasions and in certain places, carried on more successful agitation among the masses than we did. This may partly have been due to the fact that a revolutionary moment, or at a time when revolutionary recollections are still fresh, it is easier to approach the masses with tactics of sheer negation. This, however, is not an argument to prove the correctness of such tactics. At all events, there is not the least doubt that a Communist party that wishes to be the real vanguard, the advanced detachment, of the revolutionary class, of the proletariat and which, in addition wishes to learn to lead the masses, not only the proletarian, but also the non-proletarian masses of working and exploited people must know how to conduct propaganda, how to organize, and how to carry on agitation in a manner most simple and comprehensible, most clear and vivid, both to the urban, factory masses and to the rural masses.

[*10] Incidentally, this has been dealt with in an exceptionally clear, concise, precise, and Marxist way in the excellent organ of the Austrian Communist Party, The Red Banner, of March 28 and 30, 1920. (*Die Rote Fahne*, Wien, 1920, Nos. 266 and 267; L.L.: "*Ein neuer Abschnitt der deutschen Revolution*" " ["A New Stage of the German Revolution" Ed.]).

●●●

LIST OF TITLES WITH ISBN NO.

ISBN	TITLE
9788194914129	1984
9789390575220	1984 & Animal Farm (2In1)
9789390575572	1984 & Animal Farm (2In1): The International Best-Selling Classics
9789390575848	35 Sonnets
9789390575329	A Clergyman's Daughter
9789390575923	A Study In Scarlet
9789390896097	A Tale Of Two Cities
9789390896837	Abide in Christ
9789390896202	Abraham Lincoln
9789390896912	Absolute Surrender
9789390896608	African American Classic Collection
9789390575305	Aldous Huxley: The Collected Works
9789390896141	An Autobiography of M. K. Gandhi
9789390575886	Animal Farm
9789390575619	Animal Farm & The Great Gatsby (2In1)
9789390575626	Animal Farm & We
9789390896158	Anna Karenina
9789390575534	Antic Hay
9789390896165	Antony & Cleopatra
9789390896172	As I Lay Dying
9789390896226	As You like it
9789390575671	At Your Command
9789390575350	Awakened Imagination
9789390575114	Be What You Wish
9789390896233	Believe In yourself
9789390896998	Best of Charles Darwin: The Origin of Species & Autobiography
9789390896684	Best Of Horror : Dracula And Frankenstein
9789390575503	Best Of Mark Twain (The Adventures of Tom Sawyer AND The Adventures of Huckleberry Finn)
9789390896769	Black History Collection
9789390575756	Brave New World, Animal Farm & 1984 (3in1)

9789390896240	Brother Karamzov
9789390575053	Bulleh Shah Poetry
9789390575725	Burmese Days
9789390896257	Bushido
9789390896066	Can't Hurt Me
9788194914112	Chanakya Neeti: With The Complete Sutras
9789390896042	Crime and Punishment
9789390575527	Crome Yellow
9789390575046	Down and Out in Paris and London
9789390896844	Dracula
9789390575442	Emersons Essays: The Complete First & Second Series (Self-Reliance & Other Essays)
9789390575749	Emma
9789390575817	Essential Tozer Collection - The Pursuit of God & The Purpose of Man
9789390896578	Fascism What It Is and How to Fight It
9789390575688	Feeling is the Secret
9789390575190	Five Lessons
9789390575954	Frankenstein
9789390575237	Franz Kafka: Collected Works
9789390575282	Franz Kafka: Short Stories
9789390575060	George Orwell Collected Works
9789390575077	George Orwell Essays
9789390575213	George Orwell Poems
9788194914150	Greatest Poetry Ever Written Vol 1
9788194914143	Greatest Poetry Ever Written Vol 1
9789390896301	Gulliver's Travel
9789390575961	Gunaho Ka Devta
9789390575893	H. P. Lovecraft Selected Stories Vol 1
9789390575978	H. P. Lovecraft Selected Stories Vol 2
9789390896059	Hamlet
9789390575022	His Last Bow: Some Reminiscences of Sherlock Holmes
9789390896134	History of Western Philosophy
9789390575121	Homage To Catalonia

9789390896219	How to develop self-confidence and Improve public Speaking
9789390896295	How to enjoy your life and your Job
9789390575633	How to own your own mind
9789390896318	How to read Human Nature
9789390896325	How to sell your way through the life
9789390896370	How to use the laws of mind
9789390896387	How to use the power of prayer
9789390896028	How to win friends & Influence People
9788194824176	How To Win Friends and Influence People
9789390896103	Humility The Beauty of Holiness
9789390896653	Imperialism the Highest Stage of Capitalism
9789390575084	In Our Time
9789390575169	In Our Time & Three Stories and Ten poems
9789390575145	James Allen: The Collected Works
9789390896189	Jesus Himself
9789390575480	Jo's Boys
9789390896394	Julius Caesar
9789390575404	Keep the Aspidistra Flying
9789390896400	Kidnapped
9789390896424	King Lear
9789390575824	Lady Susan
9789390896455	Law of Success
9789390896264	Lincoln The Unknown
9789390575565	Little Men
9789390575640	Little Women
9788194914174	Lost Horizon
9789390896462	Macbeth
9789390896929	Man Eaters of Kumaon
9789390896523	Man The Dwelling Place of God
9789390896349	Man The Dwelling Place of God
9789390575909	Mansfield Park
9788194914136	Manto Ki 25 Sarvshreshth Kahaniya
9789390896509	Marxism, Anarchism, Communism
9789390575664	Mathematical Principles of Natural Philosophy

9788194914198	Meditations
9789390575800	Mein Kampf
9789390575794	Memory How To Develop, Train, And Use It
9789390896486	Mind Power
9789390896585	Money
9789390575039	Mortal Coils
9789390575770	My Life and Work
9789390896035	Narrative of the Life of Frederick Douglass
9789390575152	Neville Goddard: The Collected Works
9789390575985	Northanger Abbey
9789390896530	Notes From Underground
9789390896547	Oliver Twist
9789390575459	On War
9789390575541	One, None and a Hundred Thousand
9789390896554	Othelo
9789390575435	Out Of This World
9789390575015	Persuasion
9789390575510	Prayer The Art Of Believing
9789390575091	Pride and Prejudice
9789390896561	Psychic Perception
9789390575381	Rabindranath Tagore - 5 Best Short Stories Vol 2
9789390575367	Rabindranath Tagore - Short Stories (Masters Collections Including The Childs Return)
9789390575374	Rabindranath Tagore 5 Best Short Stories Vol 1 (Including The Childs Return
9789390896622	Romeo & Juliet
9789390896127	Sanatana Dharma
9789390575596	Seedtime & Harvest
9789390896639	Selected Stories of Guy De Maupassant
9789390575206	Self-Reliance & Other Essays
9789390575176	Sense and Sensibility
9789390575299	Shyamchi Aai
9789390896738	Socialism Utopian and Scientific
9789390896646	Success Through a Positive Mental Attitude
9789390575428	The Adventures of Huckleberry Finn

9789390575183	The Adventures of Sherlock Holmes
9789390575343	The Adventures of Tom Sawyer
9789390896691	The Alchemy Of Happiness
9789390575862	The Art Of Public Speaking
9789390896288	The Autobiography Of Charles Darwin
9788194914181	The Best of Franz Kafka: The Metamorphosis & The Trial
9789390575008	The Call Of Cthulhu and Other Weird Tales
9789390575107	The Case-Book of Sherlock Holmes
9789390896110	The Castle Of Otranto
9789390896745	The Communist Manifesto
9789390575589	The Complete Fiction of H. P. Lovecraft
9789390575497	The Complete Works of Florence Scovel Shinn
9789390896820	The Conquest of Breard
9789390896813	The Diary of a Young Girl
9789390896332	The Diary of a Young Girl The Definitive Edition of the Worlds Most Famous Diary
9789390575701	The Great Gatsby, Animal Farm & 1984 (3In1)
9789390575312	The Greatest Works Of George Orwell (5 Books) Including 1984 & Non-Fiction
9789390575992	The Hound of Baskervilles
9789390896707	The Idiot
9789390896714	The Invisible Man
9789390575657	The Knowledge of the holy
9789390575558	The Law & the Promise
9789390896721	The Law Of Attraction
9789390896776	The Leader in you
9789390896363	The Life of Christ
9789390896196	The Man-Eating Leopard of Rudraprayag
9789390896783	The Master Key to Riches
9789390575268	The Memoirs Of Sherlock Holmes
9789390896479	The Midsummer Night's Dream
9789390575466	The Mill On The Floss
9789390896790	The Miracles of your mind
9789390896660	The Mutual Aid A Factor in Evolution
9789390896448	The Origin of Species

9789390896905	The Peter Kropotkin Anthology The Conquest of Bread & Mutual Aid A Factor of Evolution
9789390896806	The Picture of Dorian Gray
9789390896271	The Picture of Dorian Gray
9789390575275	The Power Of Awareness
9789390896356	The Power of Concentration
9788194824169	The Power of Positive Thinking
9789390575411	The Power of the Spoken Word
9788194914105	The Power Of Your Subconscious Mind
9789390896899	The Power of Your Subconscious Mind
9789390896417	The Principles of Communism
9789390575787	The Psychology Of Mans Possible Evolution
9789390896615	The Psychology of Salesmanship
9789390575732	The Pursuit of God
9789390575398	The Pursuit of Happiness
9789390896851	The Quick and Easy Way to effective Speaking
9789390575947	The Return Of Sherlock Holmes
9789390575138	The Road To Wigan Pier
9789390896981	The Root of the Righteous
9789390575855	The Science Of Being Well
9788194914167	The Science Of Getting Rich, The Science Of Being Great & The Science Of Being Well (3In1)
9789390896011	The Screwtape Letters
9789390896073	The Screwtape Letters
9789390575336	The Secret Door to Success
9789390575695	The Secret Of Imagining
9789390896868	The Secret Of Success
9789390896431	The Seven Last Words
9789390575930	The Sign of the Four
9789390896004	The Sonnets
9789390896516	The Souls of Black Folk
9789390896875	The Sound and The Fury
9789390575244	The State and Revolution
9789390896882	The Story of My Life
9789390896936	The Story Of Oriental Philosophy

9789390896752	The Strange Case of Dr. Jekyll and Mr. Hyde
9789390896943	The Tempest
9789390575916	The Valley Of Fear
9789390575879	The Wind in the willows
9789390896080	The Wind in the willows
9789390575763	Their eyes were watching gofd
9789390575831	Three Stories
9789390896950	Twelfth Night
9789390896592	Twelve Years a Slave
9789390896677	Up from Slavery
9789390896974	Value Price and Profit
9789390896967	Wake Up and Live
9789390896493	With Christ in the School of Prayer
9789390575602	Your Faith is Your Fortune
9789390575473	Your Infinite Power To Be Rich
9789390575251	Your Word is Your Wand
9789390575718	Youth
9789391316099	A Christmas Carol
9789391316105	A Doll's House
9789391316501	A Passage to India
9789391316709	A Portrait of the Artist as a Young Man
9789391316112	A Tale of Two Cities
9789391316747	A Tear and a Smile
9789391316167	Agnes Gray
9789391316174	Alice's Adventures in Wonderland
9789391316136	Anandamath
9789391316181	Anne Of Green Gables
9789391316754	Anthem
9789391316198	Around The World in 80 Days
9789391316013	As A Man Thinketh
9789391316242	Autobiography of a Yogi
9789391316266	Beyond Good and Evil
9789391316761	Bleak House
9789391316778	Chitra, a Play in One Act
9789391316310	David Copperfield

9789391316075	Demian
9789391316785	Dubliners
9789391316051	Favourite Tales from the Arabian Nights
9789391316235	Gitanjali
9789391316068	Gravity
9789391316150	Great Speeches of Abraham Lincoln
9789391316662	Guerilla Warfare
9789391316839	Kim
9789391316822	Mother
9789391316211	My Childhood
9789391316846	Nationalism
9789391316327	Oliver Twist
9789391316853	Pygmalion
9789391316334	Relativity: The Special and the General Theory
9789391316389	Scientific Healing Affirmation
9789391316341	Sons and Lovers
9789391316587	Tales from India
9789391316372	Tess of The D'Urbervilles
9789391316396	The Awakening and Selected Stories
9789391316402	The Bhagvad Gita
9789391316303	The Book of Enoch
9789391316228	The Canterville Ghost
9789391316907	The Dynamic Laws of Prosperity
9789391316006	The Great Gatsby
9789391316860	The Hungry Stones and Other Stories
9789391316433	The Idiot
9789391316440	The Importance of Being Earnest
9789391316297	The Light of Asia
9789391316914	The Madman His Parables and Poems
9789391316457	The Odyssey
9789391316921	The Picture of Dorian Gray
9789391316464	The Prince
9789391316938	The Prophet
9789391316945	The Republic
9789391316518	The Scarlet Letter

9789391316143	The Seven Laws of Teaching
9789391316525	The Story of My Experiments with Truth
9789391316532	The Tales of the Mother Goose
9789391316549	The Thirty Nine Steps
9789391316594	The Time Machine
9789391316600	The Turn of the Screw
9789391316983	The Upanishads
9789391316617	The Yellow Wallpaper
9789391316426	The Yoga Sutras of Patanjali
9789391316990	Ulysses
9789391316624	Utopia
9789391316679	Vanity Fair
9789391316020	What Is To Be Done
9789391316686	Within A Budding Grove
9789391316693	Women in Love

www.ingramcontent.com/pod-product-compliance
Lightning Source LLC
LaVergne TN
LVHW101922220826
846093LV00009B/338

* 9 7 8 9 3 9 5 7 4 1 4 9 1 *